THE BUSINESS BEHIND LOGISTICS

Stella Eshett

Copyright © 2024

Stella Eshett

Published In Nigeria by:
Emphaloz Publishing House
www.emphaloz.com

All rights reserved.

No part of this book may be reproduced, distributed, or transmitted in any form or by any means, including photocopying, or other electronic or mechanical methods, without the prior written permission of the publisher, except in the case of brief quotations embodied in critical reviews and certain non-commercial uses permitted by copyright law

CONTENTS

Preface iv
Foreword vi
Introduction viii

Chapter One
The Foundations of Logistics *1*

Chapter Two
Supply Chain Management the Backbone of Logistics *14*

Chapter Three
Transportation and Distribution Networks the Lifeline of Logistics *29*

Chapter Four
Warehousing and Inventory Management the Pillars of Logistics Efficiency *43*

Chapter Five
Regulatory Frameworks and Compliance in Logistics *58*

Chapter Six
Technology and Innovation in Logistics *73*

Chapter Seven
Risk Management and Crisis Response in Logistics *86*

Chapter Eight
Customer Experience and Service Optimization in Logistics *99*

Chapter Nine
Global Trade and Supply Chain Expansion *112*

Chapter Ten
The Future of Logistics and Emerging Industry Trends *125*

Reviews 141

PREFACE

Logistics is the invisible engine that powers global trade, ensuring that goods, services, and raw materials flow seamlessly across industries and borders. From the movement of everyday consumer products to the coordination of complex global supply chains, logistics is the foundation of modern commerce. Yet, despite its significance, many people view logistics as merely the process of shipping and receiving, without recognizing its far-reaching impact on businesses, economies, and technological advancements.

The Business Behind Logistics is a book designed to demystify the logistics industry, revealing the strategic, operational, and technological forces that drive its success. This book provides a comprehensive exploration of logistics, covering topics such as supply chain management, risk mitigation, last-mile delivery, automation, global trade expansion, and the future of logistics. Each chapter is crafted to give readers a deep understanding of how logistics operates, the challenges it faces, and the opportunities that lie ahead.

This book is not just for logistics professionals, it is also for entrepreneurs, business leaders, students, and curious minds who want to understand the crucial role logistics plays in our everyday lives. Whether you are running a business, managing supply chains, or simply intrigued by the mechanics of global trade, this book will equip you with valuable insights into how logistics works, how it is evolving, and how you can leverage its principles for success.

Writing this book has been a journey of discovery and passion. I have drawn upon real-world experiences, industry case studies, and expert analyses to provide a clear and engaging look into the logistics sector. My goal is to bridge the gap between theory and practice, offering practical knowledge that can be applied to real-world scenarios.

I would like to extend my gratitude to the logistics professionals, industry leaders, and researchers who have contributed their insights, experiences, and expertise to enrich the contents of this book. Their contributions have made it possible to capture the depth and complexity of the logistics industry in a way that is both informative and engaging.

As you journey through the pages of *The Business Behind Logistics*, I hope you gain a newfound appreciation for the systems and people that keep the world moving. Logistics is not just about transporting goods, it is about strategy, efficiency, resilience, and innovation. This book will help you understand the past, navigate the present, and anticipate the future of logistics, equipping you with the knowledge to thrive in an increasingly interconnected world.

Welcome to the world of logistics!

FOREWORD

The world, as we know, thrives with seamless supply chains, instant access to products, and efficient movement of goods across vast distances. Behind every successful business, every fulfilled order, and every stocked shelf lies a meticulously designed logistics operation that few take the time to appreciate. Logistics is more than just a support function; it is the foundation upon which industries operate, and economies grow.

In my years of working in supply chain optimization and global trade, I have witnessed firsthand how logistics, when done right, can create a powerful competitive advantage. A well-structured logistics operation ensures that businesses reduce costs, meet customer demands with precision, and adapt to the unexpected. Conversely, poor logistics can cripple even the most promising companies, leading to supply shortages, customer dissatisfaction, and lost revenue. As businesses continue to evolve in an increasingly digital and interconnected world, logistics is no longer just about moving goods, it is about predictive analytics, real-time tracking, and sustainability.

This book, *The Business Behind Logistics*, is a timely and insightful guide that breaks down the complexities of logistics into an accessible and engaging read. Stella Eshett has meticulously explored the fundamental principles, the challenges, and the future of logistics, providing a clear roadmap for professionals, business leaders, and enthusiasts alike. Whether you are a seasoned supply chain expert or someone looking to understand how products get from point A to point B, this book will serve as an invaluable resource.

One of the things I admire most about this book is its forward-thinking approach. Logistics is not static; it is evolving faster than ever with innovations such as AI-driven forecasting, blockchain transparency, and autonomous transportation. This book does not just explain where logistics stands today, it anticipates where it is going, giving readers a strategic advantage in staying ahead of industry changes.

I highly recommend this book to anyone looking to deepen their understanding of logistics, supply chains, and the mechanics of global commerce. Whether you are an entrepreneur trying to optimize your business operations or a logistics professional seeking to refine your expertise, *The Business Behind Logistics* offers insights that will help you navigate this ever-changing field with confidence.

John Mallory

Chief Operations Officer, Global Trade Solutions

INTRODUCTION

Logistics is the invisible force that keeps the world running. It is present in every product we buy, every package we receive, and every service we consume. Without logistics, businesses would collapse, economies would stagnate, and the interconnected web of global trade would unravel. Yet, despite its crucial role, logistics often operates in the background, unnoticed by those who benefit from its efficiency. Many people see logistics as merely the process of moving goods from one place to another, but in reality, it is a complex and strategic discipline that requires meticulous planning, technological innovation, and constant adaptation to change.

This book was written to shine a light on the industry that makes modern commerce possible. *The Business Behind Logistics* is not just about trucks, warehouses, and shipping containers, it is about the art and science of making supply chains work seamlessly. Logistics determines whether a business thrives or struggles, whether customers receive their orders on time, and whether industries can scale to meet global demand. It is a field where small inefficiencies can create large disruptions, and where smart strategies can lead to game-changing advantages.

In the past, logistics was primarily about physical movement—getting goods from manufacturers to distributors and ultimately to consumers. Today, it is a technology-driven industry that relies on artificial intelligence, predictive analytics, blockchain security, and real-time tracking. The companies that succeed in logistics are those that embrace automation, invest in digital solutions, and understand the nuances of supply chain resilience. This book will take you through the evolution of logistics, from traditional supply chain models to the hyper-connected, AI-driven ecosystems of the future.

As industries shift toward global expansion, sustainability, and last-mile delivery innovations, businesses must stay ahead by understanding how logistics influences their operations. This book will guide you through the challenges and opportunities in logistics, from risk management and regulatory compliance to emerging trends like autonomous deliveries and green supply chain solutions. It will help you see logistics not as a cost center, but as a strategic advantage that can drive efficiency, reduce waste, and enhance customer experiences.

Whether you are an entrepreneur looking to streamline your supply chain, a professional working in logistics, or simply someone curious about how products reach their destinations, this book will provide valuable insights. By the time you turn the final page, you will have a deeper appreciation for the intricate networks that power global commerce, the challenges that logistics professionals navigate daily, and the exciting innovations that are shaping the future of supply chain management.

Logistics is not just about moving goods, it is about solving problems, anticipating needs, and creating seamless connections in a fast-moving world. Welcome to *The Business Behind Logistics*.

CHAPTER ONE
The Foundations of Logistics

Logistics is the backbone of modern commerce, facilitating the smooth movement of goods and services from suppliers to consumers. It is an essential aspect of any economy, influencing business efficiency, cost management, and customer satisfaction. Without logistics, businesses would struggle to manage supply chains, maintain inventories, or ensure timely delivery of products. While logistics today is a highly sophisticated system powered by technology and innovation, its roots trace back centuries to when civilizations first needed to transport goods across vast distances.

Historically, logistics was primarily associated with military operations. Armies needed efficient supply chains to transport food, weapons, and medical supplies, often determining the success or failure of military campaigns. Over time, these logistical strategies were adapted for trade and commerce, leading to the development of organized transportation networks, storage facilities, and inventory management systems. The Industrial Revolution marked a turning point in logistics, as mass production increased the need for efficient distribution systems. Railways, steamships, and mechanized warehouses transformed the way goods were transported and stored, setting the foundation for modern supply chain management.

In today's global economy, logistics extends beyond transportation and storage. It involves the integration of various processes, including procurement, warehousing, inventory management, order fulfillment, and distribution. Businesses must ensure that goods move seamlessly through these stages to maintain efficiency and profitability. Logistics is also crucial for reducing costs, as inefficient supply chains lead to wastage, higher expenses, and delays that can negatively impact customer satisfaction. Companies that master logistics gain a competitive advantage, offering faster delivery times and lower costs to their customers.

A critical aspect of logistics is transportation, which determines how quickly and efficiently goods move from one point to another. Businesses rely on different modes of transport, including road, rail, air, and sea, depending on factors such as cost, speed, and destination. Road transport is widely used for local deliveries, offering flexibility and accessibility. Rail transport is ideal for moving large quantities of goods over long distances at lower costs. Air transport, though expensive, is preferred for urgent shipments and high-value items. Sea transport remains the most economical option for international trade, handling bulk shipments across global supply chains. Each mode of transport presents unique advantages and challenges, requiring businesses to optimize their transportation strategies based on specific needs.

Warehousing plays a vital role in logistics by providing storage solutions for goods before they reach the final consumer. Effective warehousing ensures that businesses maintain the right inventory levels, preventing stock shortages or excess supply. Traditional warehouses have evolved into highly automated facilities equipped with advanced technology such as robotics, AI-driven inventory management, and real-time tracking systems. These innovations improve storage efficiency, reduce handling time, and enhance order accuracy. Companies that invest in smart warehousing solutions can respond swiftly to market demand, minimizing delays and maximizing customer satisfaction.

Inventory management is another crucial element of logistics, ensuring that businesses maintain optimal stock levels. Poor inventory control can lead to overstocking, which ties up capital and increases storage costs, or understocking, which results in missed sales and dissatisfied customers. Various inventory management techniques help businesses strike a balance, including the Just-In-Time (JIT) approach, which minimizes excess stock by synchronizing supply with demand. Other methods such as First-In-First-Out (FIFO) and Last-In-First-Out (LIFO) help businesses manage perishable and non-perishable goods effectively. The adoption of digital inventory systems has further improved stock accuracy, allowing businesses to track inventory in real-time and make data-driven decisions.

Order fulfillment is a key component of logistics, covering the entire process from receiving customer orders to delivering products. In e-commerce and retail, fast and efficient order fulfillment is crucial for maintaining customer loyalty. Companies invest in streamlined fulfillment strategies that integrate warehousing, packaging, and last-mile delivery. The last mile—the final stage of delivery from a distribution center to the customer's doorstep—remains one of the most challenging and costly aspects of logistics. Businesses continuously innovate to improve last-mile efficiency, utilizing strategies such as drone deliveries, automated sorting systems, and local distribution hubs to shorten delivery times.

Technology has revolutionized logistics, enabling businesses to optimize operations and enhance efficiency. Artificial intelligence plays a significant role in route optimization, demand forecasting, and supply chain analytics, helping companies reduce costs and improve decision-making. Blockchain technology enhances transparency and security in supply chains by providing immutable records of transactions and product movements. Automation and robotics are transforming warehousing and fulfillment processes, reducing labor costs and increasing operational speed. Additionally, big data analytics allows businesses to identify patterns and trends, improving supply chain planning and customer service. As logistics continues to evolve, companies that embrace technology will remain at the forefront of efficiency and competitiveness.

Despite its advantages, logistics faces several challenges that businesses must navigate. High transportation costs, inadequate infrastructure, regulatory complexities, and supply chain disruptions pose significant risks. In Nigeria, for instance, poor road networks, congested ports, and inconsistent government policies impact logistics efficiency. Businesses operating in such environments must develop strategies to overcome these challenges, such as leveraging technology for better route planning, forming partnerships with local logistics providers, and diversifying supply chain sources. Investing in infrastructure development and collaborating with policymakers can also help improve the overall logistics landscape.

In the modern business environment, logistics is more than just a support function—it is a strategic advantage. Companies that master logistics can reduce costs, improve customer satisfaction, and expand into new markets. Whether in manufacturing, retail, healthcare, or e-commerce, logistics plays an integral role in ensuring that businesses operate smoothly and profitably. As consumer expectations continue to rise, businesses must focus on building agile, efficient, and technology-driven logistics systems that can adapt to changing demands.

Another fundamental challenge in logistics is balancing efficiency with cost-effectiveness. Every business wants to reduce operational expenses without compromising service quality. However, achieving this balance requires careful planning and investment in modern logistics solutions. Companies must evaluate their logistics networks to identify inefficiencies and adopt strategies to improve them. For example, reducing unnecessary storage costs, optimizing delivery routes, and leveraging digital tracking systems can significantly cut logistics expenses.

The success of logistics also depends on its ability to adapt to changing market conditions. Consumer expectations are evolving rapidly, and businesses must be flexible enough to adjust their logistics operations accordingly. The rise in e-commerce, for instance, has dramatically reshaped logistics, forcing companies to enhance their order fulfillment capabilities. Consumers today expect faster delivery times, real-time tracking, and hassle-free returns. To meet these expectations, businesses are investing in logistics automation, AI-driven demand forecasting, and digital warehouse management systems.

The interconnected nature of global trade further underscores the importance of logistics. In an era where businesses source raw materials from multiple countries and distribute products to international markets, efficient logistics is essential for maintaining smooth operations. Global supply chains depend on well-coordinated logistics networks that can handle cross-border shipments, customs regulations, and international trade complexities. Companies that fail to optimize their global logistics risk facing delays, increased costs, and regulatory challenges that impact their bottom line.

In the Nigerian business landscape, logistics presents unique opportunities and challenges. The country's growing consumer market, fueled by a rising middle class and increased internet penetration, has created a surge in demand for efficient logistics services. However, infrastructure deficits, congested ports, and regulatory bottlenecks pose significant obstacles. Many businesses struggle with high transportation costs due to poor road networks and inconsistent government policies. Additionally, inefficient port operations in Lagos, which handles a significant portion of Nigeria's imports and exports, contribute to long delays and increased supply chain costs. Addressing these issues requires both private sector innovation and government intervention to improve infrastructure, streamline customs procedures, and create a more business-friendly logistics environment.

Technology is playing a pivotal role in overcoming logistics challenges in Nigeria and other emerging markets. The adoption of digital logistics platforms, GPS-enabled tracking systems, and automated warehousing solutions is improving efficiency and reducing costs. Companies like Jumia, Kobo360, and GIG Logistics are leveraging technology to enhance last-mile delivery, optimize supply chains, and provide seamless logistics services across the country. The use of mobile technology has also enabled small businesses and informal traders to access logistics services more easily, bridging the gap between suppliers and consumers.

Beyond transportation and warehousing, logistics also involves managing risks and uncertainties. Supply chain disruptions can arise from various factors, including geopolitical tensions, natural disasters, pandemics, and labor strikes. Businesses must develop contingency plans to mitigate these risks and ensure continuity in operations. Diversifying supply chain sources, maintaining safety stock, and leveraging predictive analytics can help businesses anticipate and respond to potential disruptions effectively. The COVID-19 pandemic, for instance, exposed vulnerabilities in global supply chains, forcing businesses to rethink their logistics strategies and invest in more resilient systems.

Sustainability is another critical aspect of modern logistics. As concerns about climate change and environmental impact grow, businesses are under pressure to adopt eco-friendly logistics practices. Green logistics initiatives, such as using electric vehicles, reducing packaging waste, and optimizing transportation routes to cut fuel consumption, are becoming increasingly important. Companies that prioritize sustainability not only reduce their carbon footprint but also enhance their brand reputation and appeal to environmentally conscious consumers.

Ultimately, logistics is more than just a support function, it is a strategic enabler that drives business growth and customer satisfaction. Companies that excel in logistics gain a competitive advantage by delivering superior service, reducing costs, and expanding their market reach. Whether in retail, manufacturing, healthcare, or agriculture, logistics remains a crucial element that determines operational success. As businesses continue to evolve in a digital and interconnected world, mastering logistics will be essential for staying ahead of the competition.

Logistics is an intricate and dynamic field that impacts virtually every industry, from retail and manufacturing to healthcare and agriculture. It determines how quickly products move from suppliers to customers, how efficiently businesses manage their inventory, and how companies navigate global trade complexities. While we have covered the fundamental aspects of logistics, there are still several critical components that deserve further exploration. In this section, we will examine two additional factors that shape logistics operations: the role of logistics in customer experience and the impact of globalization on modern logistics.

1.1 Logistics as a Competitive Advantage in Customer Experience

In today's fast-paced business environment, logistics is no longer just about moving goods—it has become a powerful tool for enhancing customer experience and driving brand loyalty. Consumers expect seamless shopping experiences, from easy order placement to fast and accurate deliveries. Businesses that fail to meet these expectations risk losing customers to competitors that offer more efficient logistics solutions.

The success of e-commerce giants like Amazon, Alibaba, and Jumia is largely built on their ability to provide exceptional logistics services. These companies have optimized their supply chains to ensure faster deliveries, real-time tracking, and hassle-free returns. Customers now demand transparency in logistics, expecting to receive updates on their orders at every stage of the delivery process. Businesses that fail to provide these conveniences often struggle with customer dissatisfaction and negative reviews, which can severely impact brand reputation and sales.

One of the biggest logistical challenges in customer experience is last-mile delivery. This is the final stage of the supply chain, where a product moves from a distribution center to the customer's doorstep. Last-mile delivery is often the most expensive and complex part of logistics, especially in regions with poor infrastructure or high urban congestion. Companies are constantly innovating to improve last-mile efficiency, using solutions like smart lockers, drone deliveries, and localized delivery hubs to shorten transit times. In Nigeria, logistics companies like GIG Logistics and Max.ng have introduced tech-driven approaches to enhance last-mile delivery, making it easier for businesses to reach customers across urban and rural areas.

Reverse logistics is another key aspect of customer experience. This refers to the process of handling product returns, refunds, and replacements. A smooth and customer-friendly return process enhances trust and encourages repeat purchases. Businesses must design efficient reverse logistics systems to minimize costs while ensuring customer satisfaction. In industries like fashion and electronics, where return rates are relatively high, having a well-structured return policy can be a major differentiator in a competitive market.

As logistics continues to evolve, businesses must recognize that it is not just a back-end function, it is a core part of the customer experience. Investing in efficient, tech-enabled logistics solutions helps businesses build stronger relationships with their customers, increase retention rates, and ultimately drive long-term profitability.

1.2 The Impact of Globalization on Modern Logistics

Globalization has significantly transformed logistics, making it more complex yet more critical than ever before. Businesses now operate in a borderless economy, sourcing raw materials from multiple countries, manufacturing in different regions, and selling products to consumers worldwide. While this interconnectedness offers enormous opportunities for growth, it also presents new logistical challenges that require careful navigation.

One of the most significant impacts of globalization on logistics is the expansion of international trade. Companies that previously operated within domestic markets are now competing on a global scale. This means they must develop robust logistics strategies to handle cross-border transportation, customs regulations, and international supply chain risks. The introduction of trade agreements and regional economic blocs, such as the African Continental Free Trade Area (AfCFTA), has further increased the need for efficient logistics networks that can support cross-border commerce.

Managing global supply chains requires businesses to balance multiple factors, including cost efficiency, delivery speed, and regulatory compliance. International shipping involves complex logistics planning, including route optimization, customs clearance, and coordination with multiple logistics providers. Delays in customs processing or unexpected trade restrictions can significantly impact business operations, leading to lost revenue and dissatisfied customers. To mitigate these risks, businesses must invest in supply chain visibility tools that provide real-time tracking and predictive analytics for better decision-making.

Another major challenge in global logistics is currency fluctuations and economic instability. Since international trade involves multiple currencies, businesses must factor in exchange rate risks when planning their logistics budgets. A sudden depreciation in the local currency can increase transportation costs, making imports more expensive and affecting profitability. To manage these financial risks, businesses often engage in hedging strategies or negotiate long-term contracts with logistics partners to lock in stable pricing.

Geopolitical events and trade policies also play a crucial role in global logistics. Trade wars, economic sanctions, and diplomatic tensions can disrupt supply chains, forcing businesses to adjust their logistics strategies. The U.S.-China trade war, for example, led many companies to shift manufacturing operations to alternative locations like Vietnam, India, and Mexico. Similarly, Brexit introduced new customs procedures and border checks, affecting logistics flows between the UK and the European Union. Businesses that rely on international logistics must remain agile, continuously monitoring geopolitical developments and adjusting their supply chain strategies accordingly.

Sustainability and environmental concerns have also become critical in global logistics. With rising awareness of climate change, governments and consumers are demanding more eco-friendly logistics practices. Businesses are now exploring green logistics solutions, such as reducing carbon emissions through fuel-efficient transportation, investing in electric delivery vehicles, and optimizing packaging to minimize waste. In Europe and North America, regulatory frameworks are pushing businesses toward more sustainable logistics models, and similar trends are emerging in Africa and Asia. Companies that prioritize sustainability in their logistics operations not only contribute to environmental conservation but also enhance their corporate image and appeal to socially responsible consumers.

Technology continues to play a transformative role in global logistics. Artificial intelligence, blockchain, and big data analytics are revolutionizing supply chain management, enabling businesses to make data-driven decisions and enhance efficiency. AI-powered predictive analytics help companies anticipate demand fluctuations and optimize inventory levels, reducing storage costs and preventing stock shortages. Blockchain technology enhances transparency and security in international trade, reducing fraud and ensuring authenticity in transactions. As these technologies become more widespread, businesses that embrace them will gain a competitive edge in global logistics.

Despite the challenges, globalization presents immense opportunities for businesses willing to invest in logistics excellence. Companies that master the complexities of global supply chains can expand their market reach, reduce operational costs, and enhance their competitive positioning. By leveraging technology, optimizing transportation networks, and staying ahead of regulatory changes, businesses can navigate the complexities of international logistics and build resilient supply chains for the future.

CHAPTER TWO

Supply Chain Management the Backbone of Logistics

Supply chain management is at the heart of logistics, ensuring that goods move seamlessly from suppliers to manufacturers, distributors, and finally to consumers. While logistics focuses on the movement and storage of goods, supply chain management takes a broader view, encompassing everything from raw material sourcing to demand forecasting, production planning, and inventory optimization. A well-structured supply chain reduces costs, minimizes delays, and improves overall business efficiency. Companies that master supply chain management gain a competitive advantage by delivering products faster, maintaining lower operational costs, and responding effectively to market fluctuations.

In today's interconnected world, supply chain management has become more complex yet more critical than ever before. Businesses operate in a global marketplace where disruptions in one part of the world can ripple across entire industries. The COVID-19 pandemic, for example, exposed vulnerabilities in supply chains worldwide, causing shortages of essential goods, increased freight costs, and extended delivery times. Companies that relied heavily on a single supplier or manufacturing hub faced significant challenges, forcing them to rethink their supply chain strategies.

The experience underscored the importance of building resilient and flexible supply chains that can withstand unexpected shocks.

A supply chain consists of multiple interconnected components, each playing a vital role in ensuring smooth operations. The first stage of the supply chain is **procurement**, which involves sourcing raw materials and components needed for production. Businesses must evaluate suppliers based on factors such as cost, quality, reliability, and geographic location. A strong procurement strategy ensures that companies have access to the right materials at the right time while maintaining cost efficiency. In industries like manufacturing and retail, having multiple suppliers is often a safeguard against disruptions, as it prevents over-reliance on a single source.

Once raw materials are secured, the next stage is **production planning**, where businesses determine how much to manufacture and when to do so. Efficient production planning is crucial for meeting customer demand while avoiding overproduction or stock shortages. Companies use demand forecasting techniques, powered by artificial intelligence and big data analytics, to predict future sales trends and adjust production schedules accordingly. By aligning production with demand patterns, businesses can optimize their use of resources and reduce waste.

Inventory management is another critical aspect of supply chain management. Businesses must strike a balance between keeping enough stock to meet customer demand and avoiding excess inventory that ties up capital. Poor inventory management can lead to stockouts, causing delays and dissatisfied customers, or excessive stock that increases storage costs and risks obsolescence. Strategies like the **Just-In-Time (JIT)** approach help companies minimize inventory costs by ensuring that materials and finished goods arrive precisely when needed. Other methods, such as **First-In-First-Out (FIFO)** and **Last-In-First-Out (LIFO),** help businesses manage stock rotation effectively, particularly in industries dealing with perishable goods.

The **transportation and distribution** phase is where logistics and supply chain management intersect most visibly. Once products are ready for delivery, businesses must determine the most efficient way to transport them to wholesalers, retailers, or directly to customers. Choosing the right mode of transport whether road, rail, air, or sea depends on factors such as cost, speed, and destination. Many businesses today use a multi-modal transportation strategy, combining different modes of transport to optimize delivery times and reduce costs. For instance, goods might be shipped via sea to a major port before being transported by road or rail to inland destinations.

In Nigeria and other developing markets, transportation challenges often complicate supply chain management. Poor road infrastructure, high fuel costs, and inconsistent government regulations contribute to delays and increased logistics expenses. Businesses operating in these environments must develop innovative strategies to overcome these challenges, such as using alternative transportation routes, leveraging third-party logistics providers, and investing in local distribution centers to reduce last-mile delivery costs. Companies like Kobo360 and Lori Systems are transforming supply chain management in Africa by offering digital logistics platforms that connect shippers with truck owners, improving efficiency and reducing empty truck miles.

One of the biggest challenges in supply chain management is risk management. Supply chains are vulnerable to a variety of disruptions, including natural disasters, geopolitical tensions, trade restrictions, and cyberattacks. Businesses must develop contingency plans to mitigate these risks, such as diversifying suppliers, maintaining safety stock, and adopting predictive analytics to anticipate potential disruptions. The 2021 Ever Given container ship blockage in the Suez Canal, which halted global trade for nearly a week, highlighted the need for companies to have alternative shipping routes and flexible logistics plans.

Sustainability is another growing concern in supply chain management. Consumers and governments are increasingly demanding environmentally responsible business practices. Companies are under pressure to reduce carbon emissions, minimize waste, and source raw materials ethically. Green supply chain initiatives, such as using fuel-efficient transportation, optimizing delivery routes to reduce fuel consumption, and switching to biodegradable packaging, are becoming key differentiators in the market. Many businesses are also adopting circular supply chain models, where products are designed to be recycled or repurposed at the end of their lifecycle, reducing environmental impact.

Technology plays an instrumental role in reshaping supply chain management. Artificial intelligence (AI), machine learning, blockchain, and the Internet of Things (IoT) are enabling businesses to achieve greater transparency, efficiency, and agility in their supply chains. AI-powered demand forecasting helps businesses anticipate shifts in consumer behavior, allowing them to adjust procurement and production accordingly. Blockchain technology enhances supply chain visibility by creating a secure, tamper-proof record of every transaction, reducing fraud and ensuring product authenticity. IoT-enabled sensors track shipments in real-time, providing businesses with data on location, temperature, and handling conditions, which is particularly important for industries like pharmaceuticals and food distribution.

The future of supply chain management lies in automation and digitization. Companies that embrace robotic process automation (RPA), cloud-based supply chain platforms, and AI-driven analytics will gain a competitive edge by reducing costs, improving accuracy, and responding swiftly to market demands. The adoption of digital twins, which are virtual replicas of physical supply chains, allows businesses to simulate different scenarios and optimize decision-making before implementing changes in the real world.

Supply chain management is not just about moving goods, it is about creating a seamless and efficient flow of materials, information, and capital throughout the supply network. Businesses that invest in robust supply chain strategies can improve operational efficiency, enhance customer satisfaction, and achieve sustainable growth.

Supply chain management is not just about the physical movement of goods; it is a complex, interconnected system that involves people, processes, and technology working together to ensure smooth business operations. In a world where businesses must deliver goods faster, cheaper, and more efficiently, supply chain management has become a critical factor in achieving success. Organizations that fail to manage their supply chains effectively risk delays, increased costs, and dissatisfied customers, all of which can damage their reputation and profitability.

The importance of **agility in supply chain management** cannot be overstated. Markets are dynamic, and demand patterns can shift rapidly due to factors such as seasonal trends, economic fluctuations, or unforeseen global events. Businesses must design their supply chains to be **flexible and responsive** to these changes. This involves using data-driven insights to anticipate demand fluctuations and adjusting supply chain strategies accordingly. Companies like **Amazon and Walmart** have mastered the art of supply chain agility by integrating real-time analytics, automated warehousing, and strategic partnerships with third-party logistics providers. By contrast, businesses that rely on rigid supply chain structures struggle to adapt when unexpected challenges arise.

Another crucial element of supply chain management is **collaboration and relationship management.** A supply chain is only as strong as its weakest link, meaning businesses must establish strong relationships with suppliers, logistics providers, and distribution partners. Successful supply chains operate through a network of trust, where each stakeholder is committed to delivering efficiency and quality. Companies that engage in **strategic partnerships** with their suppliers benefit from improved communication, better negotiation power, and reduced risks of supply disruptions. In the Nigerian market, businesses in industries like **agriculture and manufacturing** rely heavily on strong supplier relationships to ensure a steady flow of raw materials and production inputs.

Effective supply chain management begins with accurate demand planning. Businesses must forecast customer demand to ensure they have the right amount of stock at the right time. Poor demand planning can lead to overstocking, which ties up capital and increases storage costs, or understocking, which results in missed sales and unhappy customers. To improve demand forecasting, companies use historical sales data, market trends, and artificial intelligence-driven analytics to predict future demand patterns.

One method commonly used in demand planning is the Sales and Operations Planning (S&OP) process, which aligns supply chain activities with business goals. The S&OP process ensures that procurement, production, inventory management, and logistics work together in harmony to meet customer demand. By integrating demand forecasting with supply chain execution, businesses can reduce costs, minimize wastage, and enhance efficiency.

An example of poor demand planning was seen in the global semiconductor shortage of 2020-2021, where many industries, particularly the automotive and electronics sectors, faced massive production delays due to a lack of critical semiconductor chips. This shortage was caused by a miscalculation in demand planning, where manufacturers reduced chip orders during the pandemic, assuming demand would decline. However, as consumer demand for electronics and vehicles surged, supply chains struggled to keep up, causing price hikes and production slowdowns. This situation highlighted the importance of having a proactive demand planning strategy to prevent supply chain disruptions.

A major challenge in supply chain management is the bullwhip effect, where small fluctuations in consumer demand cause larger distortions up the supply chain. This effect occurs when businesses overreact to slight changes in demand, leading to excessive stockpiling or unnecessary production increases. The further upstream the supply chain, the more exaggerated these fluctuations become.

For example, if a retailer notices a slight increase in demand for a product, they might place larger than necessary orders with their supplier. The supplier, in turn, increases production to meet the perceived surge in demand. If this trend continues up the supply chain, manufacturers may overproduce, resulting in excess inventory and wasted resources. When demand eventually normalizes, businesses find themselves stuck with too much stock, leading to markdowns, losses, and inefficiencies.

To mitigate the bullwhip effect, companies must focus on **improving communication across the supply chain.** The use of **real-time data sharing, AI-driven forecasting, and collaborative planning tools** can help businesses align their decisions with actual market demand. By implementing **just-in-time (JIT) inventory practices, vendor-managed inventory (VMI) systems, and transparent supply chain visibility tools,** companies can reduce unnecessary fluctuations and create a more stable supply chain.

One real-world example of digital transformation in supply chain management is Walmart's use of blockchain technology. Walmart implemented blockchain-based tracking for its fresh food supply chain, allowing it to trace the journey of products from farm to shelf in seconds rather than days. This not only improved food safety but also enhanced efficiency by reducing waste and improving recall management.

Despite technological advancements, supply chain management faces several ongoing challenges. Labor shortages, geopolitical tensions, transportation disruptions, and regulatory changes continue to pose risks to global supply chains. Businesses must develop resilient supply chain strategies that allow them to adapt to these uncertainties.

One major trend shaping the future of supply chain management is reshoring and nearshoring. Many companies are shifting their manufacturing closer to home to reduce dependence on overseas suppliers. This shift is driven by factors such as rising transportation costs, supply chain disruptions, and increased emphasis on sustainability. By bringing production closer to consumer markets, businesses can reduce lead times, improve supply chain control, and minimize environmental impact.

Another key trend is the adoption of sustainable supply chain practices. Businesses are increasingly investing in eco-friendly logistics solutions, green packaging, and carbon footprint reduction strategies. Governments and consumers are demanding greater accountability in how companies' source, manufacture, and distribute goods, pushing supply chains toward greater environmental responsibility.

Supply chain management is not just a behind-the-scenes function, it is a key driver of business success in today's competitive marketplace. Companies that invest in streamlining supply chain operations, leveraging technology, and mitigating risks gain a strategic advantage by improving efficiency, reducing costs, and delivering superior customer experiences. As businesses continue to evolve in a rapidly changing world, supply chain management will play an even greater role in shaping industry trends and consumer expectations. While we have covered core aspects such as demand planning, inventory control, and supply chain risks, there are additional critical components that influence how supply chains operate effectively.

2.1 The Power of Data Analytics and AI in Supply Chain Decision-Making

In the past, supply chain management relied heavily on manual planning, experience-based decision-making, and reactive problem-solving. However, the rise of big data analytics and artificial intelligence (AI) has transformed how businesses approach supply chain optimization. The ability to analyze large volumes of real-time data enables companies to predict demand fluctuations, identify inefficiencies, and make proactive decisions that enhance overall performance.

One of the biggest benefits of AI in supply chain management is predictive analytics. By using machine learning algorithms, companies can forecast future demand with greater accuracy than traditional statistical models. For example, retailers can analyze seasonal trends, consumer purchasing behavior, and market conditions to ensure they stock the right products at the right time. This minimizes the risk of overstocking or understocking, which are common challenges that affect profitability.

AI-driven automation and robotics are also changing how warehouses and distribution centers operate. Many companies are now using automated picking and sorting systems to speed up order fulfillment, reduce errors, and enhance productivity. Robotics in warehouses, such as those used by Amazon's fulfillment centers, allow for faster processing of online orders while minimizing labor costs. These AI-powered systems can also optimize warehouse layouts to reduce travel time between product storage areas, improving efficiency and cutting down operational costs.

Another key advantage of AI in supply chain management is real-time tracking and route optimization. Logistics companies use AI to analyze traffic patterns, weather conditions, and delivery constraints to find the most efficient transportation routes. This reduces fuel costs, delivery delays, and carbon emissions. AI-powered transportation management systems (TMS) enable companies to dynamically adjust routes and schedules, ensuring deliveries arrive on time with minimal disruptions.

For example, companies like DHL and FedEx leverage AI-driven route optimization tools to track real-time package locations and predict estimated delivery times with high precision. These tools also help identify potential supply chain disruptions before they occur, allowing businesses to reroute shipments or adjust inventory allocation to avoid costly delays.

In addition to predictive analytics and automation, AI is improving supplier relationship management. Businesses can use AI-powered analytics to evaluate supplier performance, assess risks, and negotiate better contracts. AI systems analyze historical supplier data, delivery times, and quality metrics to recommend the best partners for a business's specific needs. This ensures that companies work with reliable and cost-effective suppliers, reducing the chances of supply chain bottlenecks.

The growing influence of blockchain technology in supply chains further enhances data accuracy and security. Blockchain provides a tamper-proof digital record of every transaction in the supply chain, from raw material procurement to final delivery. This not only improves transparency but also prevents fraud, counterfeiting, and product recalls. The pharmaceutical industry, for instance, uses blockchain to verify the authenticity of medicine shipments, ensuring that counterfeit drugs do not enter the market.

As businesses continue to embrace AI and data analytics, supply chains will become more resilient, agile, and responsive to market changes. Companies that leverage these technologies will gain a competitive edge by reducing costs, enhancing customer satisfaction, and improving overall supply chain visibility.

2.2 Sustainability and Ethical Sourcing in Supply Chain Management

The demand for sustainable and ethically sourced products is reshaping how businesses manage their supply chains. Consumers today are more conscious than ever about the environmental and social impact of the products they buy. Companies that fail to adopt sustainable supply chain practices risk losing customers, facing regulatory fines, and damaging their brand reputation.

Sustainability in supply chain management refers to reducing carbon emissions, minimizing waste, and sourcing materials responsibly. Businesses must ensure that every stage of their supply chain aligns with environmental, social, and governance (ESG) principles. This includes everything from using renewable energy in warehouses to implementing green packaging solutions that reduce plastic waste.

A major area of concern in supply chain sustainability is carbon footprint reduction. Transportation and logistics contribute significantly to global carbon emissions, as many businesses rely on fuel-powered vehicles, cargo ships, and airplanes to move goods. To address this, companies are exploring alternative fuel sources, electric delivery vehicles, and carbon offset programs.

For example, IKEA has committed to using 100% electric delivery trucks for last-mile deliveries in major cities, significantly reducing its carbon emissions. Similarly, logistics firms like UPS and DHL are investing in electric and hybrid vehicles to create an eco-friendlier transportation network.

Another important aspect of sustainability is reducing supply chain waste. Companies are increasingly adopting lean manufacturing and circular economy models to minimize excess inventory, recycle materials, and repurpose waste products. Many retailers now use biodegradable packaging materials instead of plastic to meet environmental standards.

Ethical sourcing is also a growing concern, particularly in industries like fashion, electronics, and agriculture. Consumers and regulatory bodies are demanding that companies ensure their suppliers comply with fair labor practices, avoid child labor, and promote safe working conditions. Businesses that engage in unethical sourcing face serious consequences, including public backlash, government sanctions, and loss of consumer trust.

A well-known case of ethical supply chain failure is the 2013 Rana Plaza disaster in Bangladesh, where a garment factory collapse killed over 1,100 workers. The incident highlighted the exploitation of cheap labor and unsafe working conditions in the global fashion supply chain. In response, many international brands pledged to improve factory conditions, enforce stricter supplier audits, and ensure ethical labor practices.

Many businesses today use supplier audits and third-party certifications to verify that their supply chains meet ethical standards. Certifications like Fair Trade, Rainforest Alliance, and B Corp help businesses demonstrate their commitment to responsible sourcing. Some companies also use blockchain technology to provide transparency in supply chains, ensuring that raw materials such as cocoa, coffee, and minerals are sourced from ethical suppliers.

Governments and regulatory bodies are also playing a role in pushing for sustainable supply chains. The European Union's Supply Chain Due Diligence Law requires companies to identify, prevent, and address human rights and environmental violations within their supply chains. Similar regulations are emerging globally, forcing businesses to adopt more responsible sourcing and production practices.

Embracing sustainability and ethical sourcing is no longer just a corporate responsibility, it is a business imperative. Companies that invest in sustainable supply chain initiatives not only reduce environmental impact but also build stronger customer relationships, enhance brand loyalty, and mitigate risks.

CHAPTER THREE
Transportation and Distribution Networks the Lifeline of Logistics

Transportation and distribution networks form the backbone of logistics, ensuring that goods move efficiently from suppliers to manufacturers, warehouses, retailers, and eventually to consumers. Without a well-structured transportation system, businesses would struggle with delays, increased costs, and supply chain inefficiencies. The ability to move goods seamlessly across different locations is what keeps economies running, businesses growing, and customers satisfied. However, managing transportation and distribution networks effectively requires careful planning, strategic decision-making, and the integration of technology to enhance speed, reduce costs, and improve reliability.

The success of any logistics operation depends on how well a company structures its transportation network, selecting the right modes of transport, optimizing delivery routes, and ensuring cost-effectiveness without compromising efficiency. Businesses must balance multiple factors such as cost, speed, reliability, security, and environmental impact when deciding on transportation strategies. A strong distribution network is what ensures that products reach their destinations on time and in the right condition, making it a critical component of supply chain management.

Transportation is one of the biggest cost drivers in logistics, often accounting for a significant portion of a company's total logistics expenses. The cost of fuel, vehicle maintenance, warehousing, labor, tolls, and government regulations all play a role in determining the efficiency and profitability of a transportation network. Poor transportation management can lead to excessive operational costs, wasted resources, and dissatisfied customers due to delayed or damaged goods. Companies that optimize their transportation networks through technology-driven solutions, route optimization strategies, and efficient load management can significantly cut costs while improving service delivery.

The effectiveness of a transportation network depends on the type of goods being transported, the distance to be covered, and the urgency of delivery. Road transport remains the most widely used method due to its flexibility, cost-effectiveness for short distances, and ability to reach even the most remote locations. Trucks, vans, and motorcycles serve different logistical needs, from long-haul freight transportation to last-mile delivery. However, road transport comes with its own set of challenges, including traffic congestion, poor road conditions, fluctuating fuel prices, and regulatory constraints that vary by region. Businesses operating in markets with poor infrastructure often face unpredictable delivery timelines, requiring them to develop contingency plans such as alternative routing, investing in fleet management technologies, and leveraging third-party logistics providers for improved efficiency.

Rail transport is a preferred option for moving large volumes of goods over long distances. It is particularly useful for transporting raw materials such as coal, steel, cement, and agricultural products in bulk. In developed countries, rail logistics is well integrated into multimodal supply chain systems, allowing for seamless transitions between train, truck, and ship transport. However, in developing countries, rail logistics often faces significant infrastructure deficits, making it a less viable option for businesses looking for speed and flexibility in their supply chain operations. The development of modern rail systems and improved cargo-handling infrastructure could significantly enhance freight transportation and reduce logistics costs in such markets.

Air freight plays a vital role in logistics, particularly for businesses that deal with high-value or time-sensitive goods. The speed of air transport makes it ideal for shipping perishable items, medical supplies, luxury goods, and urgent e-commerce orders. However, the high cost of air freight often limits its use to premium logistics services where speed is more critical than cost. Weather conditions, security risks, and airline capacity constraints can also impact the efficiency of air freight transportation. Many businesses use air freight in combination with other transport modes to strike a balance between cost and speed, ensuring that only the most urgent shipments are sent by air while less time-sensitive goods are transported by sea or road.

Sea freight remains the most cost-effective solution for transporting large quantities of goods across international borders. It is the backbone of global trade, responsible for moving raw materials, manufactured products, and industrial equipment across continents. Although sea freight is slower than air transport, its ability to handle massive shipments at a fraction of the cost makes it an attractive choice for businesses engaged in global trade. However, shipping logistics come with their own set of challenges, including long transit times, port congestion, customs clearance delays, and complex international regulations. Businesses that rely on sea freight must plan their shipments well in advance to avoid delays and ensure that their supply chains remain uninterrupted.

Multimodal and intermodal transportation strategies are increasingly being used to optimize logistics efficiency. By combining multiple transport modes, businesses can take advantage of the strengths of each method while mitigating their weaknesses. For example, a company might use sea freight to transport goods across continents, rail freight to move shipments to regional hubs, and road transport for final distribution to retailers or customers. The seamless integration of different transport modes requires sophisticated logistics planning, strong coordination between transport providers, and the use of digital tracking systems to monitor shipments in real time. Businesses that invest in intermodal logistics gain flexibility, cost savings, and enhanced service reliability.

The integration of technology into transportation and distribution networks has significantly improved logistics efficiency. GPS tracking systems, fleet management software, and real-time monitoring tools allow businesses to optimize delivery routes, track shipments, and predict delays before they happen. Artificial intelligence and machine learning are being used to analyze vast amounts of data, helping companies make smarter transportation decisions and reduce inefficiencies in their supply chains. Automation, including self-driving trucks and drone deliveries, is also emerging as a potential game-changer in logistics, particularly in last-mile delivery where speed and convenience are paramount.

Sustainability is becoming a growing concern in transportation logistics, with businesses and governments pushing for greener, more environmentally friendly transport solutions. The logistics industry is one of the largest contributors to carbon emissions, making it essential for companies to explore alternative energy sources, fuel-efficient vehicles, and route optimization techniques that reduce fuel consumption. Many businesses are investing in electric trucks, hybrid vehicles, and biofuel-powered ships to minimize their environmental impact. Sustainable transportation practices not only help companies comply with regulatory standards but also enhance their brand reputation among environmentally conscious consumers.

A well-structured distribution network is crucial for ensuring that goods reach their intended destinations efficiently. Businesses must carefully design their distribution systems to minimize transit times, reduce handling costs, and improve order fulfillment accuracy. Distribution centers play a key role in this process, serving as hubs where products are stored, sorted, and dispatched based on customer demand. The strategic placement of distribution centers in high-demand areas allows companies to reduce transportation costs and shorten delivery times. Many large retailers and e-commerce companies operate multiple distribution centers to ensure that products are always within reach of their customers, improving service speed and reliability.

Transportation and distribution networks are constantly evolving as businesses seek better ways to move goods faster, cheaper, and more efficiently. Companies that invest in logistics innovation, embrace digital transformation, and develop sustainable transportation strategies will have a competitive edge in the future of logistics. Understanding the complexities of transportation networks and adapting to new logistics trends will be key to optimizing supply chains and delivering exceptional service to customers.

One of the most significant challenges in transportation logistics is the cost factor. Fuel prices, vehicle maintenance, toll fees, labor costs, and taxes all contribute to the overall expense of moving goods. Companies that fail to optimize their transportation costs risk eroding profit margins and increasing product prices, making them less competitive in the market. To counter this, businesses are turning to technology-driven solutions that help manage costs more effectively. Route optimization software, for instance, identifies the shortest and most efficient delivery paths, reducing fuel consumption and vehicle wear and tear. Companies are also adopting load consolidation strategies, ensuring that vehicles carry full loads rather than making multiple half-empty trips, thereby cutting costs and improving efficiency.

The role of infrastructure development cannot be overlooked in transportation logistics. Poorly maintained roads, congested highways, inefficient ports, and inadequate railway systems can slow down deliveries and increase operational costs. In developed nations, advanced road networks, high-speed rail systems, and state-of-the-art port facilities facilitate smooth logistics operations. However, in regions where infrastructure development is lagging, businesses must develop alternative strategies to mitigate transportation bottlenecks. In Nigeria, for example, road transportation dominates the logistics sector, but poor road conditions and traffic congestion in major cities like Lagos create significant challenges. As a solution, businesses are investing in regional distribution hubs, enabling them to store goods closer to customers and reduce reliance on long-haul transportation.

Another critical aspect of transportation logistics is security and risk management. The movement of goods is vulnerable to various risks, including theft, damage, hijacking, and accidents. High-value shipments, such as electronics, pharmaceuticals, and luxury goods, require enhanced security measures to prevent losses. Businesses are integrating real-time tracking systems, tamper-proof packaging, and insurance coverage into their logistics strategies to mitigate risks. In regions with high cargo theft rates, companies are employing security escorts, controlled access warehouses, and automated tracking systems to ensure the safety of goods in transit. The use of blockchain technology also helps gain traction, providing tamper-proof records of shipments, transactions, and cargo handling, reducing fraud and improving trust in the logistics ecosystem.

A major transformation in transportation and distribution networks is the rise of last-mile delivery innovation. Last-mile delivery refers to the final leg of the supply chain, where goods are transported from a distribution center or local warehouse to the end customer. This stage is often the most challenging and expensive part of the logistics process, accounting for a significant percentage of total delivery costs. Urban congestion, unpredictable traffic patterns, and inefficient address systems further complicate last-mile logistics. To address these challenges, businesses are turning to alternative delivery solutions, including electric scooters, autonomous delivery robots, and drone technology. Companies like Amazon and UPS are actively testing drone delivery systems, reducing delivery times and minimizing carbon emissions. In

Nigeria, logistics startups such as Kwik and MAX.ng are leveraging motorcycle couriers to bypass traffic congestion and ensure faster last-mile delivery.

E-commerce has been a major driver of last-mile delivery transformation, with customers demanding same-day and next-day delivery options. To keep up with this shift, businesses are adopting micro-fulfillment centers, small urban warehouses that store high-demand products closer to consumers. These centers significantly reduce delivery times and improve service reliability. Additionally, smart locker systems emerge as a viable solution, allowing customers to collect their orders from secure self-service lockers at their convenience, eliminating the need for direct home deliveries.

Beyond urban logistics, rural transportation networks present unique challenges. Poor road infrastructure, limited transport options, and low population density make rural logistics less profitable for traditional carriers. However, businesses are exploring innovative distribution models to improve rural reach. In some regions, companies are partnering with local transport operators, postal services, and informal logistics networks to extend their supply chain into remote areas. Mobile technology is also playing a key role, enabling rural consumers to place orders via digital platforms while businesses use data analytics to forecast demand and optimize delivery schedules.

Sustainability in transportation is another pressing issue that businesses must address. The logistics industry is a major contributor to carbon emissions, fuel consumption, and environmental degradation. As a result, businesses are under increasing pressure to adopt eco-friendly logistics solutions that minimize environmental impact. Many companies are transitioning to electric and hybrid vehicles, reducing their reliance on fossil fuels. Others are optimizing fuel efficiency through AI-driven route planning, ensuring that vehicles take the shortest, most fuel-efficient paths. Some logistics providers are investing in alternative fuel sources, such as hydrogen-powered trucks and biofuels, reducing their carbon footprint.

Shipping companies are also exploring ways to make sea freight more environmentally friendly. The International Maritime Organization (IMO) has implemented stricter emissions regulations, requiring shipping lines to reduce sulfur content in fuel and adopt cleaner technologies. Some shipping companies are experimenting with wind-assisted propulsion, solar energy, and LNG-powered vessels, paving the way for greener maritime logistics. In the aviation sector, sustainable aviation fuel (SAF) is gaining traction, offering a lower-carbon alternative to traditional jet fuel.

The integration of digital technologies is transforming transportation networks, making them smarter and more efficient. The rise of Internet of Things (IoT) sensors enables businesses to track shipments in real time, monitor cargo conditions, and predict potential disruptions. Predictive analytics and artificial intelligence are allowing companies to anticipate demand fluctuations, optimize fleet utilization, and reduce unnecessary expenses. Cloud-based transportation management systems (TMS) are streamlining logistics operations, providing businesses with real-time visibility into their supply chains and helping them make data-driven decisions.

As businesses navigate the complexities of transportation logistics, collaboration and partnerships are becoming increasingly important. Logistics companies, technology firms, and government agencies are working together to develop infrastructure, create smart logistics hubs, and implement regulatory reforms that support efficient transportation networks. Public-private partnerships are being explored to invest in road and rail expansion projects, improve port efficiency, and integrate multimodal transport systems that enhance connectivity.

In the future, transportation and distribution networks will continue to evolve, driven by advancements in automation, electrification, AI-powered logistics, and sustainability initiatives. Businesses that embrace innovation, invest in technology, and optimize their transportation strategies will remain competitive, agile, and resilient in an increasingly demanding logistics landscape.

The success of any business depends on the efficiency of its transportation and distribution networks. These networks connect every link in the supply chain, ensuring that goods move smoothly from manufacturers to consumers. A well-structured transportation system is critical for reducing operational costs, improving customer satisfaction, and maintaining supply chain reliability. Businesses must continuously optimize their logistics strategies to adapt to changing market demands, technological advancements, and sustainability concerns. While we have covered the fundamental aspects of transportation logistics, two key areas deserve further exploration: the impact of geopolitical and regulatory challenges on transportation networks and the role of artificial intelligence (AI) in revolutionizing freight and logistics.

3.1 Geopolitical and Regulatory Challenges in Transportation Networks

Transportation logistics is heavily influenced by geopolitical factors, trade policies, and government regulations. Businesses that operate across borders must navigate a complex web of customs procedures, tariffs, trade restrictions, and international transportation laws. Global events such as trade wars, diplomatic tensions, and conflicts can disrupt transportation routes, causing unexpected delays and increasing costs. For companies engaged in international trade, staying informed about geopolitical risks is essential for maintaining supply chain resilience.

A major example of how geopolitics affects transportation is the U.S.-China trade war, which led to increased tariffs on imported goods and forced businesses to reconfigure their supply chains. Companies that previously relied on Chinese manufacturers had to shift production to alternative locations such as Vietnam, India, and Mexico to avoid high import duties. This shift disrupted established transportation routes, requiring businesses to develop new logistics strategies and establish alternative trade corridors.

Another geopolitical factor that influences transportation is maritime trade disruptions. The Suez Canal blockage in 2021, caused by the Ever-Given container ship running aground, demonstrated how a single event could halt global trade for weeks, delaying billions of dollars' worth of goods. The incident forced businesses to rethink their reliance on single shipping routes and invest in contingency plans such as diversifying shipping lanes and using alternative transit hubs.

Customs regulations and border control policies also play a crucial role in transportation logistics. Import and export laws vary from country to country, and businesses must ensure compliance to avoid penalties, cargo seizures, or delays. Stringent customs clearance procedures can increase lead times and add unexpected costs to international shipments. For instance, Nigeria's complex customs procedures and frequent policy changes often create bottlenecks at major ports, causing delays in cargo clearance. To navigate these challenges, businesses are investing in customs brokerage services, digital trade platforms, and AI-powered compliance tools that streamline regulatory processes and reduce paperwork burdens.

Regional trade agreements and economic blocs also shape transportation logistics. Agreements such as the African Continental Free Trade Area (AfCFTA) aim to reduce trade barriers, improve cross-border transportation, and create a more integrated logistics network across Africa. By simplifying customs procedures and standardizing trade regulations, such agreements encourage businesses to expand their reach and optimize transportation efficiencies. However, businesses must stay informed about policy updates, tariff structures, and regulatory changes to fully leverage the benefits of such trade agreements.

3.2 Artificial Intelligence and the Future of Freight Logistics

The rapid adoption of artificial intelligence (AI) is transforming transportation and distribution networks, making logistics smarter, faster, and more efficient. AI-driven technologies are helping businesses optimize route planning, fleet management, demand forecasting, and warehouse automation, reducing operational costs and improving delivery accuracy. Companies that embrace AI in logistics gain a significant competitive advantage by enhancing efficiency, reducing human error, and improving supply chain visibility.

One of the most significant applications of AI in freight logistics is route optimization. AI-powered systems analyze real-time traffic data, weather conditions, and delivery constraints to determine the most efficient transportation routes. This reduces fuel consumption, minimizes delays, and ensures on-time deliveries. Logistics giants such as DHL, UPS, and FedEx use AI-driven route planning software to dynamically adjust delivery schedules and prevent supply chain disruptions. In urban logistics, AI-driven traffic prediction models help businesses avoid congested roads and optimize last-mile delivery routes.

Another major AI-driven innovation in freight logistics is autonomous delivery systems. Companies such as Amazon and Tesla are developing self-driving trucks and autonomous drones to revolutionize cargo transportation. Autonomous trucks, equipped with AI-powered navigation systems, can operate continuously without driver fatigue, improving delivery efficiency and reducing labor costs. Drone deliveries, already being tested for last-mile logistics, have the potential to reduce delivery times and reach remote areas that are difficult to access with traditional vehicles.

AI is also transforming predictive maintenance in transportation logistics. By analyzing data from vehicle sensors, AI can detect mechanical issues before they lead to breakdowns, allowing businesses to perform preventive maintenance and reduce downtime. Predictive maintenance systems help logistics companies avoid unexpected vehicle failures, extend the lifespan of transport assets, and improve overall fleet reliability.

AI-powered demand forecasting is another game-changer in transportation logistics. Machine learning algorithms analyze historical sales data, seasonal trends, and external factors such as economic shifts to predict future transportation needs. This allows businesses to plan optimal inventory levels, allocate transportation resources efficiently, and prevent supply chain bottlenecks. E-commerce companies use AI-powered demand forecasting to anticipate peak shopping seasons, ensuring that their transportation networks can handle increased order volumes.

In warehouse distribution, AI is being used to automate sorting, packing, and inventory management. AI-powered robots in fulfillment centers can identify products, arrange shipments, and load trucks with minimal human intervention. Automated logistics hubs enable businesses to process orders faster, reduce labor costs, and increase supply chain efficiency. Retail giants like Walmart and Alibaba have invested heavily in AI-powered warehouse automation, streamlining their logistics operations and setting new standards for global supply chain efficiency.

AI is also revolutionizing freight matching platforms, connecting businesses with available carriers to maximize truck utilization and minimize empty return trips. Freight matching algorithms analyze shipment requirements, available transport capacity, and real-time carrier locations to match cargo with the most suitable transport provider. This optimizes logistics efficiency, reduces emissions, and lowers costs for businesses engaged in bulk freight movement.

CHAPTER FOUR

Warehousing and Inventory Management the Pillars of Logistics Efficiency

Warehousing and inventory management are fundamental components of the logistics ecosystem, serving as the bridge between production and distribution. The ability to store, manage, and track goods efficiently determines how well businesses meet customer demands, minimize operational costs, and ensure smooth supply chain operations. A well-structured warehousing system provides businesses with faster order fulfillment, reduced stock losses, and optimized inventory control, all of which contribute to a competitive edge in the marketplace.

The importance of warehousing has grown significantly with the rise of e-commerce, global trade expansion, and just-in-time manufacturing. Businesses are no longer simply storing goods; they manage dynamic fulfillment centers, automated distribution hubs, and real-time inventory systems that require precision, speed, and technology integration. Poorly managed warehouses lead to delayed deliveries, stock imbalances, increased holding costs, and dissatisfied customers. To thrive in today's logistics landscape, businesses must adopt smart warehousing strategies and implement inventory management systems that enhance accuracy, reduce waste, and improve supply chain visibility.

The role of a warehouse extends beyond storage—it is a strategic asset that determines how efficiently products move through the supply chain. The placement of warehouses affects transportation costs, delivery speed, and order processing efficiency. Businesses must consider factors such as proximity to suppliers, customer demand locations, accessibility to transportation networks, and storage conditions when setting up their warehousing infrastructure. Leading companies like Amazon and Alibaba have built extensive warehouse networks across multiple regions, ensuring that customers receive orders in the shortest time possible.

Inventory management, on the other hand, focuses on maintaining the right balance of stock to meet demand without incurring excess holding costs. Holding too much inventory ties up capital and increases storage costs, while insufficient stock leads to missed sales opportunities and customer dissatisfaction. Businesses must adopt data-driven inventory management techniques to anticipate demand fluctuations, optimize stock levels, and prevent supply chain disruptions.

Warehouses today are no longer just static storage facilities. They are highly automated, technology-driven logistics hubs designed to improve efficiency, accuracy, and speed. The integration of robotics, artificial intelligence, machine learning, and IoT (Internet of Things) sensors has revolutionized warehousing operations. Automated picking and sorting systems enable businesses to process orders faster, while AI-driven inventory tracking ensures real-time stock monitoring, demand forecasting, and replenishment planning.

Businesses must also optimize warehouse layout and space utilization to maximize efficiency and minimize handling costs. Poor warehouse organization leads to delays in order processing, increased labor costs, and operational inefficiencies. An optimized warehouse layout includes clearly defined picking areas, logical shelving arrangements, strategically placed high-demand items, and automated retrieval systems that speed up product movement. Cross-docking strategies, where inbound shipments are transferred directly to outbound vehicles without long-term storage, further reduce handling time and improve order fulfillment speed.

Inventory accuracy is one of the biggest challenges in warehousing. Manual stock tracking methods are prone to human errors, leading to discrepancies between recorded inventory and actual stock levels. Businesses must invest in barcode scanning, RFID (Radio Frequency Identification) technology, and cloud-based inventory management systems to improve tracking accuracy and reduce stock variances. RFID technology, for instance, allows businesses to scan multiple items simultaneously, enabling real-time tracking and automated inventory reconciliation.

Just-in-time (JIT) inventory management is a strategy that helps businesses reduce excess stock while ensuring products are available when needed. By synchronizing procurement with production and demand, businesses can minimize storage costs, reduce waste, and enhance efficiency. However, JIT requires strong supplier relationships, accurate demand forecasting, and agile logistics capabilities to prevent stock shortages or delays. Toyota's production system is one of the best-known examples of JIT inventory management, allowing the company to operate with minimal excess inventory while maintaining a smooth production flow.

The concept of safety stock is also critical in inventory management. Businesses maintain a buffer stock to protect against unexpected demand spikes, supplier delays, or transportation disruptions. Determining the right level of safety stock involves analyzing historical sales data, lead time variability, and demand patterns to ensure that businesses are prepared for uncertainties without overstocking.

Another essential aspect of inventory management is demanding forecasting. Companies must analyze past sales trends, market conditions, seasonal fluctuations, and economic indicators to predict future demand accurately. The use of big data analytics, machine learning algorithms, and AI-driven predictive models has significantly improved businesses' ability to forecast demand, preventing stockouts and reducing waste. Walmart, for example, uses AI-powered demand forecasting tools to optimize inventory levels across its vast global supply chain, ensuring that the right products are always available in the right locations.

Reverse logistics is another important yet often overlooked component of warehouse and inventory management. Businesses must have efficient systems in place to handle product returns, repairs, recycling, and disposal. The rise in e-commerce has made returns management a critical aspect of logistics, as customers expect hassle-free return policies. A poorly managed reverse logistics system leads to inventory losses, increased operational costs, and negative customer experiences. Companies must implement streamlined return processes, automated restocking systems, and sustainable disposal methods to minimize waste and recover value from returned goods.

The future of warehousing and inventory management is centered on automation, digitalization, and sustainability. Warehouses are increasingly integrating AI-powered robotics, automated guided vehicles (AGVs), drone-based inventory tracking, and smart conveyor systems to enhance efficiency. Sustainable warehousing practices, such as solar-powered distribution centers, eco-friendly packaging, and energy-efficient storage solutions, are also gaining traction as businesses seek to reduce their environmental footprint.

Cold chain logistics, a specialized form of warehousing, is essential for industries such as pharmaceuticals, food, and biotechnology, where temperature-sensitive products require precise climate control. Companies must invest in temperature-monitoring systems, real-time tracking, and insulated storage solutions to ensure product integrity and regulatory compliance. The COVID-19 vaccine distribution highlighted the critical role of cold storage logistics, as vaccines had to be transported and stored at extremely low temperatures to maintain efficacy.

In today's fast-moving logistics environment, businesses cannot afford to rely on outdated warehousing and inventory management methods. The integration of technology, data-driven decision-making, and automated logistics systems is no longer a luxury but a necessity for businesses looking to scale operations and meeting evolving consumer demands. Companies that invest in smart warehousing solutions, AI-driven inventory optimization, and sustainable logistics practices will gain a competitive advantage in the modern supply chain landscape.

The effectiveness of warehousing and inventory management directly impacts a company's ability to fulfill orders, maintain cash flow, and scale operations. While warehousing ensures that goods are stored safely and systematically, inventory management dictates how well businesses balance stock levels to meet demand without incurring unnecessary costs. The synergy between these two functions determines how efficiently a supply chain operates. As consumer expectations rise and businesses expand their global reach, warehouses are evolving from simple storage facilities to highly sophisticated logistics hubs that rely on automation, artificial intelligence, and real-time data analytics to maintain precision, speed, and efficiency.

One of the most pressing challenges in warehousing is the cost of maintaining storage space. Warehousing costs encompass rent, utilities, security, labor, and equipment maintenance. Businesses must optimize warehouse space to reduce overhead costs while maximizing storage capacity. Poor warehouse design leads to inefficient use of space, causing bottlenecks, unnecessary movement of goods, and delayed order processing. To counter this, companies use vertical storage solutions, dynamic racking systems, and automated retrieval technologies to make the best use of available space.

The strategic placement of warehouses is another critical factor in logistics. Businesses must consider proximity to suppliers, major transportation hubs, and customer locations when setting up storage facilities. A well-located warehouse minimizes transportation costs, shortens lead times, and improves service levels. For example, large e-commerce companies strategically place fulfillment centers in high-demand regions, ensuring that products reach customers faster while reducing last-mile delivery costs.

A growing trend in warehousing is on-demand warehousing, where businesses rent storage space based on seasonal demand rather than committing to long-term leases. This model provides flexibility, especially for retailers and e-commerce businesses experiencing fluctuating inventory needs. Companies like Flexe and Stord offer on-demand warehouse networks, allowing businesses to scale storage capacity up or down based on demand, reducing unnecessary costs and improving agility.

Warehouse efficiency also depends on picking and packing strategies. Order fulfillment speed is critical in industries such as retail, manufacturing, and healthcare, where delayed shipments can impact business operations and customer satisfaction. Traditional warehouses relied on manual picking methods, where workers searched for and retrieved items. However, modern fulfillment centers integrate automated picking systems, conveyor belt sorting, and AI-driven packing algorithms to accelerate order processing and reduce human error.

One of the biggest challenges businesses face in inventory management is stock shrinkage, the loss of inventory due to theft, misplacement, damage, or accounting errors. Stock shrinkage leads to financial losses, operational inefficiencies, and inaccurate demand forecasting. Companies implement barcode scanning, RFID tracking, and AI-driven inventory monitoring to improve stock accuracy and reduce shrinkage. These technologies ensure that inventory records are continuously updated, minimizing discrepancies between physical stock and recorded inventory levels.

The role of real-time inventory visibility is becoming increasingly crucial in logistics. Businesses that lack real-time insights into stock levels struggle with overstocking, understocking, and order fulfillment delays. Cloud-based inventory management systems provide centralized visibility across multiple warehouses, suppliers, and distribution centers, enabling businesses to track stock movements, automate replenishment, and improve supply chain responsiveness.

A critical aspect of warehousing and inventory management is cycle counting, a process where businesses periodically count a portion of inventory instead of conducting a full physical count. Cycle counting helps identify discrepancies, detect theft, and ensure inventory accuracy without causing major disruptions in warehouse operations. Companies that implement continuous cycle counting improve inventory control, reducing the risk of supply chain disruptions.

For businesses dealing with perishable goods, warehouse climate control is an essential factor in inventory management. Products such as food, pharmaceuticals, and chemicals require temperature-controlled storage to maintain product integrity. Cold chain logistics ensure that goods are stored and transported at optimal temperatures, reducing spoilage and ensuring compliance with health and safety regulations. Smart sensors and IoT-enabled temperature monitoring devices alert businesses to temperature fluctuations, humidity changes, and potential spoilage risks, enabling quick corrective action to prevent product loss.

The importance of safety and security in warehousing cannot be ignored. Warehouses store valuable goods, making them prime targets for theft and unauthorized access. Companies implement security surveillance systems, controlled access points, biometric authentication, and alarm systems to safeguard inventory. Additionally, workplace safety measures, such as fire suppression systems, ergonomic lifting equipment, and employee safety training programs, reduce the risk of warehouse accidents and ensure compliance with occupational safety regulations.

Reverse logistics, an integral part of inventory management, plays a crucial role in handling returns, product recalls, and refurbishments. With the rise of e-commerce, customer returns have become a major challenge for businesses, requiring efficient systems to manage returned inventory. Poor reverse logistics processes lead to financial losses, stock obsolescence, and increased waste. Businesses implement automated return processing, AI-driven quality inspections, and resale strategies to maximize the value of returned products and minimize waste.

The future of warehousing is being shaped by robotics, AI, and predictive analytics. AI-powered algorithms analyze historical sales data, consumer behavior patterns, and economic indicators to predict demand, allowing businesses to adjust inventory levels proactively. Robotics is playing an increasingly significant role in warehouse automation, with autonomous mobile robots (AMRs) and robotic picking arms handling tasks that traditionally required human intervention. Companies like Amazon, Walmart, and Ocado are heavily investing in AI-driven fulfillment centers, drastically reducing order processing times and improving warehouse efficiency.

Sustainability is also becoming a priority in warehouse operations. Businesses are integrating solar energy, eco-friendly packaging materials, and waste reduction initiatives into their warehouse management strategies. Sustainable warehousing not only reduces environmental impact but also lowers energy costs and improves brand reputation. Companies that adopt green logistics practices gain a competitive advantage by appealing to environmentally conscious consumers and meeting regulatory compliance standards.

The concept of warehouse decentralization is expected to reshape logistics strategies. Instead of relying on centralized mega warehouses, businesses are shifting toward regional micro-fulfillment centers to reduce transportation distances and meet rising consumer demand for faster deliveries. This model enhances supply chain agility, allowing businesses to serve customers more efficiently while reducing last-mile logistics costs.

The evolution of on-demand warehousing, AI-driven inventory management, and automation is transforming how businesses store, track, and move goods. Companies that invest in advanced warehousing solutions, data-driven inventory strategies, and sustainable logistics practices will be better positioned to compete in an increasingly complex and fast-moving market.

4.1 Warehousing

The effectiveness of warehousing and inventory management directly impacts a company's ability to fulfill orders, maintain cash flow, and scale operations. While warehousing ensures that goods are stored safely and systematically, inventory management dictates how well businesses balance stock levels to meet demand without incurring unnecessary costs. The synergy between these two functions determines how efficiently a supply chain operates. As consumer expectations rise and businesses expand their global reach, warehouses are evolving from simple storage facilities to highly sophisticated logistics hubs that rely on automation, artificial intelligence, and real-time data analytics to maintain precision, speed, and efficiency.

One of the most pressing challenges in warehousing is the cost of maintaining storage space. Warehousing costs encompass rent, utilities, security, labor, and equipment maintenance. Businesses must optimize warehouse space to reduce overhead costs while maximizing storage capacity. Poor warehouse design leads to inefficient use of space, causing bottlenecks, unnecessary movement of goods, and delayed order processing. To counter this, companies use vertical storage solutions, dynamic racking systems, and automated retrieval technologies to make the best use of available space.

The strategic placement of warehouses is another critical factor in logistics. Businesses must consider proximity to suppliers, major transportation hubs, and customer locations when setting up storage facilities. A well-located warehouse minimizes transportation costs, shortens lead times, and improves service levels. For example, large e-commerce companies strategically place fulfillment centers in high-demand regions, ensuring that products reach customers faster while reducing last-mile delivery costs.

A growing trend in warehousing is on-demand warehousing, where businesses rent storage space based on seasonal demand rather than committing to long-term leases. This model provides flexibility, especially for retailers and e-commerce businesses experiencing fluctuating inventory needs. Companies like Flexe and Stord offer on-demand warehouse networks, allowing businesses to scale storage capacity up or down based on demand, reducing unnecessary costs and improving agility.

Warehouse efficiency also depends on picking and packing strategies. Order fulfillment speed is critical in industries such as retail, manufacturing, and healthcare, where delayed shipments can impact business operations and customer satisfaction. Traditional warehouses relied on manual picking methods, where workers searched for and retrieved items. However, modern fulfillment centers integrate automated picking systems, conveyor belt sorting, and AI-driven packing algorithms to accelerate order processing and reduce human error.

One of the biggest challenges businesses face in inventory management is stock shrinkage, the loss of inventory due to theft, misplacement, damage, or accounting errors. Stock shrinkage leads to financial losses, operational inefficiencies, and inaccurate demand forecasting. Companies implement barcode scanning, RFID tracking, and AI-driven inventory monitoring to improve stock accuracy and reduce shrinkage. These technologies ensure that inventory records are continuously updated, minimizing discrepancies between physical stock and recorded inventory levels.

The role of real-time inventory visibility is becoming increasingly crucial in logistics. Businesses that lack real-time insights into stock levels struggle with overstocking, understocking, and order fulfillment delays. Cloud-based inventory management systems provide centralized visibility across multiple warehouses, suppliers, and distribution centers, enabling businesses to track stock movements, automate replenishment, and improve supply chain responsiveness.

4.2 Inventory Management

A critical aspect of warehousing and inventory management is cycle counting, a process where businesses periodically count a portion of inventory instead of conducting a full physical count. Cycle counting helps identify discrepancies, detect theft, and ensure inventory accuracy without causing major disruptions in warehouse operations. Companies that implement continuous cycle counting improve inventory control, reducing the risk of supply chain disruptions.

For businesses dealing with perishable goods, warehouse climate control is an essential factor in inventory management. Products such as food, pharmaceuticals, and chemicals require temperature-controlled storage to maintain product integrity. Cold chain logistics ensure that goods are stored and transported at optimal temperatures, reducing spoilage and ensuring compliance with health and safety regulations. Smart sensors and IoT-enabled temperature monitoring devices alert businesses to temperature fluctuations, humidity changes, and potential spoilage risks, enabling quick corrective action to prevent product loss.

The importance of safety and security in warehousing cannot be ignored. Warehouses store valuable goods, making them prime targets for theft and unauthorized access. Companies implement security surveillance systems, controlled access points, biometric authentication, and alarm systems to safeguard inventory. Additionally, workplace safety measures, such as fire suppression systems, ergonomic lifting equipment, and employee safety training programs, reduce the risk of warehouse accidents and ensure compliance with occupational safety regulations.

Reverse logistics, an integral part of inventory management, plays a crucial role in handling returns, product recalls, and refurbishments. With the rise of e-commerce, customer returns have become a major challenge for businesses, requiring efficient systems to manage returned inventory. Poor reverse logistics processes lead to financial losses, stock obsolescence, and increased waste. Businesses implement automated return processing, AI-driven quality inspections, and resale strategies to maximize the value of returned products and minimize waste.

The future of warehousing is being shaped by robotics, AI, and predictive analytics. AI-powered algorithms analyze historical sales data, consumer behavior patterns, and economic indicators to predict demand, allowing businesses to adjust inventory levels proactively. Robotics is playing an increasingly significant role in warehouse automation, with autonomous mobile robots (AMRs) and robotic picking arms handling tasks that traditionally required human intervention. Companies like Amazon, Walmart, and Ocado are heavily investing in AI-driven fulfillment centers, drastically reducing order processing times and improving warehouse efficiency.

Sustainability is also becoming a priority in warehouse operations. Businesses are integrating solar energy, eco-friendly packaging materials, and waste reduction initiatives into their warehouse management strategies. Sustainable warehousing not only reduces environmental impact but also lowers energy costs and improves brand reputation. Companies that adopt green logistics practices gain a competitive advantage by appealing to environmentally conscious consumers and meeting regulatory compliance standards.

CHAPTER FIVE

Regulatory Frameworks and Compliance in Logistics

Regulatory frameworks and compliance form the backbone of global logistics, dictating how businesses transport goods across borders, manage supply chains, and adhere to international trade laws. Every movement of goods whether by air, sea, rail, or road is subject to an extensive set of legal requirements designed to ensure safety, fair trade, and environmental responsibility. Failure to comply with these regulations can lead to hefty fines, shipment delays, reputational damage, and even legal action. Understanding the intricacies of logistics compliance is not only necessary for avoiding penalties but also for ensuring smooth and efficient operations in an increasingly interconnected world.

Businesses engaged in international trade must comply with customs regulations that dictate how goods are classified, valued, and documented. Customs authorities enforce duties and tariffs based on the Harmonized System (HS) code classification; a globally recognized numerical system used to categorize products. Misclassification of goods can result in fines, delays, or increased import taxes, making it imperative for companies to assign the correct HS codes to their shipments. Additionally, businesses must provide detailed commercial invoices, packing lists, and certificates of origin to prove the legitimacy of their trade activities. These documents help customs authorities assess duties, ensure compliance with trade agreements, and prevent the circulation of restricted or counterfeit goods.

One of the biggest challenges in customs compliance is navigating the constantly evolving landscape of trade policies. Governments frequently update tariff structures, introduce new trade restrictions, and revise import/export regulations, forcing businesses to stay informed or risk being caught off guard. Many companies invest in customs brokerage services and trade compliance software to automate classification, generate accurate documentation, and stay updated on regulatory changes. The use of digital trade platforms has significantly reduced paperwork and streamlined the customs clearance process, allowing businesses to process shipments faster and reduce administrative costs.

Beyond customs compliance, businesses must also adhere to strict transportation and safety regulations that vary by country and industry. The movement of hazardous materials, perishable goods, and fragile items requires special handling procedures to ensure product integrity and public safety. Logistics companies that transport chemicals, explosives, pharmaceuticals, or biohazardous materials must comply with hazardous materials (HAZMAT) regulations that govern labeling, packaging, and storage requirements. Non-compliance can lead to catastrophic accidents, environmental damage, and legal consequences, making it essential for businesses to train employees in safe handling procedures and invest in secure packaging solutions.

Environmental compliance is another critical component of logistics regulations, as governments impose stricter policies to reduce the carbon footprint of transportation and supply chain operations. Many countries have introduced fuel efficiency standards, carbon emission taxes, and restrictions on single-use packaging materials to encourage greener logistics practices. Businesses are under pressure to transition to sustainable logistics models by adopting fuel-efficient transportation methods, investing in electric delivery vehicles, and optimizing supply chain routes to reduce emissions. Companies that fail to comply with environmental regulations may face penalties, increased operational costs, and reputational risks, particularly as consumers become more environmentally conscious and demand greater accountability from corporations.

Trade agreements and free trade zones play a significant role in shaping logistics regulations, influencing how businesses structure their supply chains and access global markets. Free trade agreements eliminate or reduce tariffs between member countries, allowing businesses to trade more competitively by lowering import costs and simplifying customs procedures. Companies that understand and leverage trade agreements such as the African Continental Free Trade Area (AfCFTA), the United States-Mexico-Canada Agreement (USMCA), and the European Union Customs Union can gain a strategic advantage by optimizing supply chains and expanding their market reach. Free trade zones further enhance logistics efficiency by allowing businesses to store, process, or manufacture goods in designated areas without immediate customs duties. These zones serve as key logistics hubs, enabling companies to re-export products to different markets with reduced regulatory burdens.

As logistics becomes increasingly digitized, technology is playing a crucial role in ensuring compliance with regulatory frameworks. Businesses are leveraging artificial intelligence, blockchain, and digital customs platforms to automate trade compliance, track shipments in real time, and enhance transparency in supply chains. AI-powered compliance software analyzes regulatory data, identifies potential risks, and alerts businesses to new trade policies that may impact their operations. Blockchain technology enhances supply chain security by creating tamper-proof records of transactions, reducing fraud, and ensuring that all stakeholders have access to accurate, verifiable trade data. Digital trade management systems integrate customs documentation, trade analytics, and automated compliance checks, enabling businesses to process shipments faster and reduce the risk of errors.

Despite the advancements in regulatory compliance technology, businesses must remain proactive in managing legal risks associated with logistics. Compliance is not a one-time task but an ongoing process that requires continuous monitoring, staff training, and collaboration with legal experts. Many companies establish compliance teams dedicated to monitoring trade regulations, conducting internal audits, and liaising with regulatory authorities to address compliance issues before they escalate. Non-compliance not only results in financial penalties but also disrupts supply chains, damages relationships with trade partners, and creates uncertainty in business operations.

For logistics companies, compliance extends beyond customs and environmental regulations to include labor laws and workplace safety standards. Warehouses, distribution centers, and transportation fleets must comply with labor laws that govern working hours, wages, and employee benefits. Businesses that violate labor regulations face legal action, strikes, and reputational damage, particularly in industries where worker exploitation and unsafe working conditions have come under scrutiny. Many companies invest in ethical sourcing programs, supply chain audits, and fair labor certifications to ensure compliance with labor laws and demonstrate corporate responsibility.

In an era where supply chain disruptions can have global ripple effects, businesses that prioritize regulatory compliance gain a competitive edge by minimizing risks and enhancing operational efficiency. Compliance is no longer just a legal requirement; it is a strategic imperative that determines how smoothly goods move through supply chains and how well businesses adapt to changing market conditions. Companies that invest in compliance technology, build strong relationships with regulatory bodies, and stay ahead of policy changes will be better equipped to navigate the complexities of global trade.

The regulatory landscape governing logistics is complex and ever evolving, shaped by factors such as trade policies, safety standards, environmental mandates, and geopolitical developments. As businesses expand their supply chains across multiple jurisdictions, compliance becomes more than just a legal requirement—it becomes a strategic necessity for sustaining smooth operations, avoiding financial penalties, and maintaining a good reputation in the industry. Companies that fail to adhere to logistics regulations face not only monetary fines but also shipment seizures, contract terminations, and supply chain disruptions that could have long-term consequences. Regulatory compliance is a key differentiator in logistics, separating well-managed, risk-averse companies from those prone to inefficiencies and legal disputes.

One of the most critical aspects of logistics compliance is import and export control, which governs how goods are moved across borders. Governments impose strict trade laws to regulate cross-border transactions, ensuring that businesses pay the appropriate tariffs, follow security protocols, and meet product standards. Many of these laws are established to protect local industries, prevent the circulation of counterfeit goods, and uphold international trade agreements. Non-compliance with import/export laws can result in delays, product recalls, and costly legal battles. Companies engaged in international trade must work closely with customs officials, freight forwarders, and compliance specialists to ensure that their shipments align with tariff classifications, restricted goods lists, and documentation requirements.

The enforcement of trade compliance laws varies from country to country, creating an additional challenge for businesses that operate across multiple regions. Some countries maintain strict protectionist policies, imposing high tariffs and quotas to discourage foreign imports, while others have liberalized trade regimes that facilitate free movement of goods. Businesses must stay informed about changes in global trade policies, particularly in the wake of political shifts, trade wars, and economic sanctions that can alter market dynamics overnight. For example, during the U.S.-China trade war, tariffs on hundreds of product categories were revised, forcing businesses to restructure their supply chains, renegotiate contracts, and seek alternative manufacturing partners to avoid excessive costs.

Regulatory frameworks in logistics also extend to intellectual property (IP) protection and anti-counterfeiting laws. The global supply chain is vulnerable to counterfeit goods, particularly in industries such as pharmaceuticals, electronics, luxury fashion, and automotive parts. Governments impose strict intellectual property laws to prevent the importation and distribution of counterfeit products that could harm consumers and legitimate businesses. Companies must conduct thorough due diligence on their suppliers, verify authenticity through track-and-trace systems, and comply with IP regulations to protect their brands from being associated with illicit trade. Advanced technologies such as blockchain, AI-powered product authentication, and serialization codes are helping businesses safeguard their supply chains against counterfeiting risks.

Beyond trade policies, compliance in logistics also involves health and safety regulations that ensure the protection of workers, consumers, and the environment. Warehouses, transportation fleets, and distribution centers must comply with occupational safety standards to prevent workplace accidents, hazardous material spills, and equipment failures that could jeopardize operations. Governments enforce stringent occupational health and safety (OHS) laws that require logistics companies to implement workplace safety training, emergency response plans, and hazard management systems. Failure to comply with these regulations can lead to lawsuits, operational shutdowns, and damage to a company's public image.

Environmental compliance is another growing concern in logistics, as governments and regulatory bodies enforce stricter laws to reduce carbon emissions, fuel consumption, and waste generation. Many countries have implemented green logistics policies that require businesses to adopt fuel-efficient vehicles, eco-friendly packaging, and carbon offset programs. Companies that fail to comply with environmental laws may face carbon taxes, emissions penalties, and restrictions on fleet operations. Logistics providers are increasingly investing in electric trucks, solar-powered warehouses, and route optimization technology to minimize their environmental impact and meet regulatory requirements.

Another important area of logistics compliance is data protection and cybersecurity laws, particularly for businesses that manage digital supply chain systems, IoT-connected warehouses, and online freight management platforms. Governments have enacted data privacy regulations such as the General Data Protection Regulation (GDPR) in the European Union and the California Consumer Privacy Act (CCPA) to protect sensitive information from cyber threats. Logistics companies must ensure that their customer data, shipment records, and tracking information are safeguarded against cyberattacks, unauthorized access, and data breaches. Cybersecurity compliance involves encryption protocols, secure cloud storage, and risk assessment procedures to protect supply chain data from digital threats.

Businesses must also be aware of financial compliance regulations, particularly when dealing with international trade finance, foreign exchange transactions, and anti-money laundering (AML) laws. Many logistics companies engage in cross-border payments, freight financing, and credit agreements, all of which require compliance with financial reporting and transparency laws. Regulatory bodies monitor financial transactions to prevent fraud, tax evasion, and illicit trade activities, requiring businesses to maintain accurate records of their financial operations. Non-compliance with financial regulations can lead to frozen assets, banking restrictions, and loss of business partnerships, making it crucial for logistics firms to implement strong financial governance frameworks.

The complexity of logistics compliance has led many businesses to adopt compliance management software and AI-driven regulatory monitoring systems to stay ahead of evolving laws. These digital solutions provide real-time updates on regulatory changes, automated trade documentation, and risk assessment tools that help companies streamline their compliance processes. Businesses that fail to leverage technology for compliance management often struggle with manual errors, regulatory blind spots, and inefficient documentation handling that increase the likelihood of legal complications.

In an era of global supply chain disruptions, trade uncertainties, and heightened regulatory scrutiny, compliance is no longer optional, it is a competitive necessity. Companies that build strong compliance frameworks, integrate digital compliance solutions, and engage with regulatory bodies proactively will gain a strategic advantage in navigating complex trade environments. Regulatory compliance is not just about avoiding fines, it is about building trust, enhancing operational efficiency, and ensuring long-term sustainability in logistics operations.

5.1 Labor and Human Rights Compliance in Logistics Operations

The logistics industry relies heavily on human labor, from warehouse workers and truck drivers to port operators and customs officials. With the rise of global trade, businesses have come under increasing scrutiny regarding labor conditions, fair wages, and workplace safety standards. Many countries enforce strict labor laws that regulate working hours, employee benefits, and occupational health and safety to prevent worker exploitation and ensure fair treatment. Companies that fail to comply with labor laws risk lawsuits, operational disruptions, and reputational damage that can negatively impact their brand image and customer trust.

A major concern in logistics compliance is forced labor and unethical employment practices within supply chains. Governments and regulatory bodies have implemented strict policies to eliminate exploitative labor practices, particularly in industries that rely on low-cost manufacturing and distribution. The United Nations, International Labour Organization (ILO), and various human rights organizations have called for greater accountability in global supply chains to prevent child labor, forced labor, and inhumane working conditions. Countries such as the United States, Canada, and European Union members have passed laws requiring businesses to conduct human rights due diligence (HRDD) to ensure that their supply chains are free from labor exploitation.

The U.S. Uyghur Forced Labor Prevention Act (UFLPA) and the United Kingdom's Modern Slavery Act are examples of legal frameworks aimed at ensuring ethical labor practices. Companies found to have links to forced labor in their supply chains face import bans, legal action, and severe financial penalties. To comply with these regulations, businesses must conduct supplier audits, employee welfare assessments, and ethical sourcing certifications to verify that their logistics partners adhere to fair labor standards. Many companies now use blockchain and AI-driven verification systems to track labor practices within their supply chains, ensuring transparency and accountability.

Warehouse and transportation worker safety is another critical compliance issue in logistics. Many logistics hubs operate around the clock, handling heavy machinery, hazardous materials, and high-pressure workloads that increase the risk of workplace accidents. Governments impose occupational health and safety (OHS) regulations to protect workers from injuries, exposure to harmful substances, and unsafe working conditions. In many countries, logistics companies must adhere to standards set by organizations such as the Occupational Safety and Health Administration (OSHA) in the United States or the Health and Safety Executive (HSE) in the UK. Compliance with these safety standards requires businesses to implement workplace safety training programs, equipment maintenance protocols, and emergency response systems to prevent accidents and ensure a secure working environment.

Another key issue in labor compliance is driver work-hour regulations in road freight transportation. Many countries enforce maximum working hours, rest break requirements, and electronic logging device (ELD) mandates to prevent fatigue-related accidents among truck drivers. Logistics companies must monitor driver schedules to ensure compliance with regulations that limit driving hours and mandate adequate rest periods. Failure to comply with these laws can result in penalties, vehicle impoundment, and liability claims in the event of accidents.

The push for ethical labor compliance extends beyond human rights concerns to include gender equality, diversity, and inclusion in logistics operations. Many companies are adopting policies to promote equal pay, non-discriminatory hiring practices, and career advancement opportunities for women and underrepresented groups in logistics. Businesses that prioritize workplace diversity and gender equity not only comply with labor laws but also improve organizational performance, employee retention, and brand reputation.

5.2 The Impact of Geopolitical Shifts on Logistics Regulations

Geopolitical developments play a crucial role in shaping logistics regulations, influencing trade agreements, customs procedures, and transportation policies. Changes in government leadership, diplomatic tensions, and international conflicts can alter trade routes, disrupt supply chains, and impose new regulatory burdens on businesses. Logistics companies must remain agile and adaptable to shifting geopolitical landscapes to minimize risks and maintain operational continuity.

One of the most significant geopolitical factors affecting logistics is trade sanctions and embargoes. Countries frequently impose economic sanctions against nations, industries, or individuals involved in activities that violate international laws or pose security threats. Businesses engaged in global trade must ensure that they do not conduct transactions with sanctioned entities or ship restricted goods to embargoed regions. Non-compliance with trade sanctions can lead to severe penalties, asset seizures, and loss of export privileges. Companies use sanctions screening tools and compliance software to verify that their supply chain partners are not listed on restricted trade lists issued by organizations such as the U.S. Office of Foreign Assets Control (OFAC) and the European Union Sanctions List.

Another major geopolitical influence on logistics compliance is tariff wars and trade disputes. Trade conflicts between major economies, such as the U.S.-China trade war, Brexit, and Russia-Ukraine sanctions, have led to fluctuating tariffs, supply chain bottlenecks, and shifting trade alliances. Businesses that rely on international sourcing must stay updated on changes in import duties, preferential trade agreements, and tariff adjustments to mitigate financial risks. Many companies adopt supply chain diversification strategies to reduce dependency on any single country or region, ensuring greater resilience in the face of trade disruptions.

Political instability and regional conflicts also impact logistics compliance, particularly in countries experiencing civil unrest, economic instability, or government regime changes. Logistics companies must assess political risk factors, supply chain security vulnerabilities, and potential regulatory overhauls when operating in politically unstable regions. Many businesses purchase political risk insurance to protect against unforeseen disruptions that could impact cargo shipments, foreign investments, and cross-border trade agreements.

International logistics regulations are also influenced by climate change policies and global environmental agreements. Governments worldwide are pushing for greener supply chain practices by enforcing stricter emissions targets, carbon taxes, and sustainable transportation initiatives. Businesses must adapt to regulatory shifts in fuel efficiency standards, electric vehicle mandates, and pollution control measures to maintain compliance with evolving environmental laws. Logistics companies that fail to comply with climate-related regulations may face higher operational costs, restricted fleet usage, and negative public perception.

The expansion of regional trade blocs and economic partnerships also shapes logistics compliance requirements. Organizations such as the African Continental Free Trade Area (AfCFTA), the Association of Southeast Asian Nations (ASEAN), and the European Union Customs Union create standardized trade policies that simplify logistics within their respective regions. Businesses that take advantage of these trade agreements benefit from reduced tariffs, expedited customs clearances, and streamlined regulatory compliance processes. Companies that fail to align their logistics strategies with regional trade agreements risk higher operational costs and trade barriers.

As global trade becomes more interconnected, businesses must integrate geopolitical intelligence, risk assessment tools, and international compliance management systems into their logistics operations. Companies that proactively monitor geopolitical developments, trade law changes, and regulatory updates will be better equipped to navigate complex trade environments while minimizing legal and financial risks.

CHAPTER SIX

Technology and Innovation in Logistics

Technology and innovation have revolutionized the logistics industry, transforming traditional supply chain operations into highly efficient, data-driven ecosystems. The rapid evolution of digital tools, automation, and artificial intelligence has not only improved operational efficiency but also enhanced visibility, accuracy, and speed in transportation, warehousing, and inventory management. In an era where consumers demand faster deliveries, seamless tracking, and sustainability, businesses must integrate advanced technologies into their logistics strategies to stay competitive. The shift toward smart logistics, predictive analytics, and real-time monitoring is reshaping how goods move across global supply chains, reducing inefficiencies, and increasing profitability.

One of the most significant technological advancements in logistics is the adoption of Artificial Intelligence (AI) and Machine Learning (ML). AI-driven logistics platforms analyze vast amounts of data to optimize route planning, demand forecasting, fleet management, and warehouse automation. AI-powered demand forecasting enables businesses to anticipate customer needs, adjust inventory levels, and reduce waste, ensuring that products are always available at the right time and in the right quantities. Machine learning algorithms continuously improve these predictions, allowing businesses to fine-tune their logistics strategies based on real-time market trends.

Automation has also played a transformative role in warehousing and order fulfillment. Traditional warehouses, once dependent on manual labor for stocking, picking, and packing, are now integrating robotics, automated storage and retrieval systems (AS/RS), and autonomous mobile robots (AMRs) to streamline operations. These innovations have significantly reduced order processing times, minimized human errors, and improved warehouse efficiency. Retail giants like Amazon, Walmart, and Alibaba have embraced fully automated warehouses where robots handle everything from inventory movement to order fulfillment, ensuring faster delivery turnaround.

The Internet of Things (IoT) has further enhanced supply chain visibility by enabling real-time tracking of shipments, assets, and fleet vehicles. IoT-enabled sensors, RFID tags, and GPS tracking devices provide real-time data on cargo location, temperature, humidity, and handling conditions. This level of transparency is particularly crucial for industries such as pharmaceuticals, food, and electronics, where product integrity depends on strict environmental controls. Logistics companies use IoT technology to monitor shipment conditions, prevent cargo theft, and proactively address delays or disruptions.

Blockchain technology is another game-changer in logistics, providing secure, transparent, and tamper-proof records of transactions across the supply chain. Traditional supply chains often suffer from data discrepancies, fraudulent activities, and inefficiencies due to reliance on paper-based documentation. Blockchain eliminates these challenges by creating a decentralized ledger system where all stakeholders, manufacturers, suppliers, logistics providers, and customers—can access a single, immutable source of truth. This innovation has been particularly useful in customs clearance, contract management, and verifying product authenticity, reducing paperwork and speeding up trade processes. Many global corporations, including Maersk and IBM, have implemented blockchain-based supply chain solutions to enhance trust, security, and operational efficiency.

E-commerce growth has driven the need for last-mile delivery innovations, as businesses strive to meet rising consumer expectations for fast and flexible shipping options. The emergence of autonomous delivery vehicles, drones, and smart lockers has transformed the way goods are delivered to end customers. Companies like Amazon, UPS, and FedEx are experimenting with drone deliveries to reduce transportation costs and reach remote areas more efficiently. Similarly, autonomous electric delivery robots are being deployed in urban areas to handle small package deliveries, cutting down on labor costs and carbon emissions.

Another major innovation reshaping logistics is the integration of Big Data and Predictive Analytics. Businesses collect and analyze massive amounts of logistics data to identify inefficiencies, optimize supply chain performance, and enhance decision-making. Predictive analytics allows companies to anticipate demand fluctuations, potential bottlenecks, and weather-related disruptions, ensuring proactive solutions are implemented before problems arise. Retailers and logistics providers leverage big data insights to personalize delivery options, reduce shipping costs, and improve customer satisfaction.

Sustainability has become a driving force in logistics innovation, with businesses adopting eco-friendly solutions to reduce carbon footprints, optimize fuel consumption, and implement greener supply chain practices. Governments worldwide are enforcing stricter environmental regulations, prompting companies to invest in electric trucks, alternative fuels, energy-efficient warehouses, and carbon offset programs. The logistics industry is embracing green logistics initiatives such as route optimization, zero-emission vehicles, and sustainable packaging solutions to align with global sustainability goals. Major logistics companies, including DHL, UPS, and Maersk, have committed to achieving net-zero carbon emissions by integrating renewable energy sources and electrifying their fleets.

Cloud-based logistics management systems have also streamlined supply chain coordination by providing real-time data access, automated workflows, and seamless collaboration between stakeholders. Cloud computing allows businesses to manage their logistics operations remotely, track shipments across multiple regions, and analyze performance metrics in real time. Companies using cloud-based logistics platforms benefit from faster decision-making, improved efficiency, and reduced IT infrastructure costs.

Drones and unmanned aerial vehicles (UAVs) are playing an increasingly important role in logistics, particularly in areas with limited road infrastructure or natural disaster zones. In remote regions, drones are being used to deliver medical supplies, essential goods, and emergency relief aid where traditional delivery methods are impractical. Companies like Zipline and Matternet have successfully deployed drone delivery networks in countries such as Rwanda, Ghana, and India, showcasing the potential for expanding drone-based logistics solutions worldwide.

Augmented Reality (AR) and Virtual Reality (VR) are also making their way into logistics, particularly in warehouse training, inventory management, and order fulfillment. AR-powered smart glasses assist warehouse workers by displaying real-time picking instructions, optimizing navigation within storage facilities, and improving accuracy in order processing. VR is being used for simulated warehouse training programs, allowing employees to gain hands-on experience without disrupting daily operations. These technologies enhance productivity, reduce onboarding times, and improve workforce efficiency in logistics environments.

Cybersecurity has become a pressing concern as logistics companies transition to digitized supply chain management. The rise of ransomware attacks, data breaches, and cyber threats has made it essential for businesses to implement strong cybersecurity frameworks, secure data encryption protocols, and risk mitigation strategies to protect sensitive logistics data. Companies must ensure that cloud-based logistics platforms, IoT devices, and blockchain networks are safeguarded against cyber vulnerabilities to prevent supply chain disruptions and data theft.

The rapid advancement of 5G connectivity is set to revolutionize logistics operations by enabling ultra-fast data transfer, low-latency communication, and enhanced IoT integration. With 5G-powered logistics networks, businesses can achieve real-time inventory tracking, predictive maintenance for fleet vehicles, and seamless automation of smart warehouses. The deployment of 5G technology will improve logistics efficiency, reduce downtime, and enhance overall supply chain connectivity.

As logistics technology continues to evolve, businesses must stay ahead of emerging trends and invest in cutting-edge innovations that improve efficiency, transparency, and sustainability. Companies that embrace AI-driven automation, blockchain security, IoT-enabled tracking, and green logistics solutions will remain competitive in a rapidly changing marketplace.

Digital twins are one of the most transformative innovations in modern logistics. A digital twin is a virtual replica of a physical logistics system, including warehouses, supply chains, transportation fleets, and distribution centers. These virtual models allow businesses to simulate, monitor, and optimize real-world logistics operations in real-time, making data-driven decisions that enhance efficiency and reduce costs.

By creating a digital replica of a warehouse, for example, companies can analyze inventory movements, storage capacity, and picking efficiency without physically disrupting operations. Businesses can run simulations to test new warehouse layouts, robotic automation, and workflow optimizations before implementing changes in the real world. This approach reduces risks, minimizes operational downtime, and ensures that warehouses operate at maximum efficiency.

In transportation, digital twins allow businesses to monitor fleet performance, vehicle wear and tear, fuel consumption, and route optimization in real time. Logistics companies can simulate traffic patterns, weather conditions, and road congestion scenarios to determine the most efficient delivery routes. This technology is particularly beneficial for last-mile logistics, where small route optimizations can significantly reduce fuel costs and delivery times.

Digital twins also enhance supply chain visibility by allowing companies to predict bottlenecks, simulate supply chain disruptions, and model alternative sourcing strategies in response to changing market conditions. This capability is crucial in a world where pandemics, trade disputes, and natural disasters can disrupt global supply chains overnight. Businesses that leverage digital twin technology gain real-time predictive insights, increased supply chain resilience, and enhanced decision-making power that gives them a competitive advantage.

As logistics technology advances, the industry is moving toward autonomous operations and smart transportation networks that require minimal human intervention. Autonomous logistics refers to the use of self-driving trucks, unmanned aerial vehicles (UAVs), and robotic warehouse systems to manage supply chains with greater efficiency, precision, and cost-effectiveness.

Self-driving trucks are expected to revolutionize freight transportation by reducing driver dependency, optimizing fuel efficiency, and increasing delivery speed. Companies like Tesla, Waymo, and Embark are investing heavily in autonomous trucking solutions that use AI-powered navigation, real-time sensor mapping, and vehicle-to-infrastructure (V2I) communication to transport goods safely and efficiently. The adoption of autonomous trucks will reduce labor costs, minimize human errors, and extend driving hours beyond current regulatory limits, making long-haul freight transport more efficient.

Unmanned aerial vehicles (UAVs), commonly known as drones, are gaining traction as an alternative delivery solution, particularly in remote locations and high-traffic urban areas. Drones can bypass road congestion, deliver small packages quickly, and operate with lower emissions than traditional delivery vehicles. Companies like Amazon Prime Air, Zipline, and UPS Flight Forward are developing drone delivery networks that promise faster last-mile fulfillment, reduced logistics costs, and enhanced delivery accessibility.

In warehouse operations, autonomous mobile robots (AMRs) are transforming order fulfillment and inventory management. Unlike traditional conveyor belt systems, AMRs navigate warehouse environments independently, using AI-driven sensors and real-time mapping to retrieve items, transport goods, and optimize warehouse workflows. These robots improve picking accuracy, reduce labor-intensive tasks, and enhance overall warehouse efficiency.

The rise of smart transportation networks is also reshaping how goods move across supply chains. Smart logistics networks leverage real-time traffic data, AI-powered route optimization, and vehicle connectivity to improve delivery speed and reliability. Many cities are integrating smart traffic management systems that communicate with logistics fleets to provide real-time route updates, minimizing delivery delays caused by congestion, road closures, and accidents.

Blockchain technology plays a crucial role in ensuring the security and transparency of autonomous logistics networks. By using blockchain-based smart contracts, logistics companies can automate transactions, verify delivery milestones, and prevent fraud in transportation agreements. This innovation reduces reliance on manual paperwork and enhances trust between supply chain partners.

As the adoption of autonomous logistics expands, businesses must address regulatory challenges, infrastructure readiness, and cybersecurity risks. Many countries still lack clear legislation governing self-driving trucks and drone deliveries, creating uncertainty about liability, insurance policies, and safety regulations. Additionally, as logistics systems become more digitized, companies must strengthen their cybersecurity defenses to protect against hacking, data breaches, and operational disruptions.

Technology and innovation continue to push the logistics industry toward greater efficiency, automation, and sustainability. The integration of digital twins, AI-driven automation, IoT-enabled tracking, and blockchain security is transforming traditional supply chain operations into intelligent, data-driven ecosystems. Businesses that invest in real-time analytics, autonomous logistics, and predictive logistics strategies will remain at the forefront of an industry that is evolving faster than ever before.

The logistics of the future will be hyper-connected, AI-driven, and optimized for maximum efficiency, speed, and sustainability. Companies that embrace emerging technologies will be able to anticipate disruptions, reduce operational costs, and provide superior customer experiences. As the industry moves toward self-driving freight, drone deliveries, and smart warehouses, logistics professionals must adapt to the changing technological landscape to maintain a competitive edge.

6.1 The Role of 5G and Edge Computing in Logistics Connectivity

The logistics industry relies heavily on real-time data exchange, which requires fast, reliable, and low-latency connectivity. Traditional networks often struggle to handle the vast amount of data generated by IoT-enabled supply chains, smart warehouses, and fleet management systems. The introduction of 5G technology and edge computing is transforming logistics by providing faster communication speeds, reduced latency, and enhanced connectivity for real-time decision-making.

5G technology enables logistics companies to operate fully connected supply chains where vehicles, warehouses, and tracking systems communicate seamlessly. The increased bandwidth and reduced latency of 5G allow logistics providers to track shipments in real-time with greater accuracy, reduce communication delays between distribution centers, and improve fleet performance through real-time diagnostics. This advancement is particularly useful for businesses managing cross-border logistics, e-commerce fulfillment, and high-speed delivery services.

With 5G-enabled IoT sensors, businesses can monitor cargo conditions, optimize fleet routes, and ensure just-in-time inventory replenishment without interruptions caused by network congestion. In transportation logistics, 5G connectivity enhances autonomous vehicle performance by enabling instantaneous data transmission between self-driving trucks, smart traffic systems, and logistics hubs. This allows for faster response times, improved route optimization, and safer navigation in urban environments.

Edge computing complements 5G by processing logistics data closer to the source rather than relying on centralized cloud servers. This reduces network latency and enables real-time analytics at ports, warehouses, and transport hubs. In a logistics warehouse, edge computing can process barcode scans, robotic picking instructions, and real-time inventory updates without the delays associated with cloud-based computing. Similarly, in fleet management, edge computing enables instantaneous tracking, predictive maintenance alerts, and fuel efficiency monitoring, improving overall logistics performance.

The combination of 5G and edge computing enhances last-mile logistics by supporting AI-powered delivery bots, drone-assisted package drop-offs, and smart locker systems for seamless consumer experiences. Businesses that adopt these technologies will benefit from faster deliveries, reduced logistics costs, and improved operational agility.

6.2 The Integration of Sustainable Technology Solutions in Smart Logistics

Sustainability is becoming a core focus in logistics as businesses and governments push for greener supply chain solutions. With increasing concerns about carbon emissions, fuel efficiency, and environmental impact, logistics companies are leveraging sustainable technology solutions to create eco-friendly, low-carbon supply chains.

One of the key advancements in sustainable logistics is the adoption of electric and hydrogen-powered trucks. Traditional diesel-powered freight vehicles are being phased out in favor of electric trucks that reduce carbon emissions, lower fuel costs, and operate more efficiently. Companies like Tesla, Volvo, and Daimler have introduced long-range electric trucks that support sustainable freight transportation without compromising on speed and cargo capacity. Hydrogen fuel cell technology is also gaining traction as an alternative power source for logistics fleets, particularly for long-haul and heavy-duty transport applications.

Green warehousing is another major shift in sustainable logistics. Businesses are investing in energy-efficient warehouses, solar-powered distribution centers, and AI-driven climate control systems to reduce energy consumption. Smart lighting, automated temperature regulation, and IoT-enabled energy monitoring help businesses cut down on electricity usage and minimize their carbon footprint. Some logistics providers are integrating rainwater harvesting systems and biodegradable packaging solutions to further enhance their sustainability goals.

The rise of circular supply chains is also influencing logistics sustainability. Instead of relying on a traditional linear model where products are manufactured, used, and discarded, businesses are implementing circular supply chain strategies that focus on product reuse, recycling, and remanufacturing. Logistics companies are optimizing reverse logistics solutions to manage returns, refurbishment, and material recovery, reducing overall waste and improving resource efficiency.

Blockchain technology is playing a crucial role in ensuring sustainable sourcing and ethical supply chains. Companies can use blockchain to verify the authenticity of sustainable products, track carbon emissions, and enforce environmental compliance across supply chain networks. Businesses that integrate blockchain with sustainability tracking systems can provide consumers and regulatory bodies with transparent, immutable proof of their eco-friendly logistics practices.

With increased pressure from regulatory agencies and environmentally conscious consumers, logistics companies must embrace sustainable innovations to remain competitive. The adoption of alternative energy sources, AI-driven route optimization, and eco-friendly packaging materials is reshaping the logistics industry to reduce environmental impact, improve operational efficiency, and align with global sustainability targets.

CHAPTER SEVEN

Risk Management and Crisis Response in Logistics

Risk management is a fundamental pillar of logistics, as businesses operate in an environment filled with uncertainties that can disrupt supply chains at any moment. From natural disasters and geopolitical conflicts to cyberattacks and supply shortages, logistics operations are constantly exposed to risks that threaten efficiency, profitability, and customer satisfaction. Companies that lack proactive risk management strategies often face shipment delays, financial losses, and reputational damage, whereas businesses that invest in resilient logistics frameworks and crisis response plans can navigate disruptions with agility and confidence.

As global supply chains grow more interconnected, the impact of disruptions can be widespread and severe. A factory shutdown in China, a port strike in Europe, or a cyberattack on a freight management system can send shockwaves across industries, causing cascading delays and inventory shortages. The COVID-19 pandemic highlighted the vulnerabilities of logistics networks, with businesses scrambling to secure alternative suppliers, reroute shipments, and manage fluctuating demand. To prevent future disruptions, companies must adopt robust risk management frameworks that include contingency planning, predictive analytics, and diversified sourcing strategies.

One of the most pressing risks in logistics is natural disasters, including hurricanes, earthquakes, floods, and wildfires. These catastrophic events can damage infrastructure, shut down ports, disrupt transportation networks, and delay shipments for weeks or months. Businesses that rely on just-in-time inventory systems are particularly vulnerable, as even a short disruption can result in stockouts and revenue losses. To mitigate the impact of natural disasters, logistics companies invest in real-time weather tracking, disaster preparedness training, and flexible supply chain routing that allows shipments to be rerouted through unaffected regions.

Geopolitical risks also pose significant challenges for logistics operations. Trade wars, economic sanctions, political instability, and military conflicts can lead to border closures, tariff hikes, customs delays, and restricted access to key trade routes. Businesses operating in global markets must continuously monitor political developments, trade agreements, and regional security risks to anticipate disruptions and adjust logistics strategies accordingly. Many companies develop multi-sourcing strategies, regional distribution hubs, and alternative shipping routes to reduce dependence on any single country or region.

Cybersecurity threats are an emerging risk in logistics, as digital transformation increases reliance on cloud-based logistics platforms, IoT-connected supply chains, and AI-powered inventory systems. Cybercriminals target logistics networks with ransomware attacks, data breaches, and phishing schemes that can disrupt operations, steal sensitive information, and halt freight movement.

A cyberattack on a shipping line or port authority can cause global supply chain paralysis, as seen in the 2017 NotPetya ransomware attack that crippled Maersk's operations and cost the company over $300 million in damages. To protect against cyber threats, logistics companies must implement advanced cybersecurity protocols, multi-factor authentication, real-time threat monitoring, and employee training programs to enhance digital security.

Another major risk in logistics is supply chain fraud and cargo theft. Criminal organizations target high-value shipments, counterfeit trade routes, and unsecured warehouses to intercept goods before they reach their intended destinations. In some regions, cargo theft is a multi-billion-dollar industry, with stolen goods being resold on black markets or illegally reintroduced into legitimate supply chains. Businesses mitigate cargo theft risks by investing in GPS tracking, AI-powered shipment monitoring, tamper-proof packaging, and secure transportation partnerships. Blockchain technology is also being leveraged to enhance supply chain transparency, verify product authenticity, and prevent fraudulent transactions.

Pandemic-related disruptions have reshaped logistics risk management, as businesses were forced to rethink inventory planning, supplier relationships, and emergency response strategies during the COVID-19 crisis. The pandemic caused factory shutdowns, raw material shortages, port congestion, and labor force reductions, exposing weaknesses in global supply chains. Businesses that depended on a single-source supplier model struggled to meet demand, while those with multi-sourcing strategies and flexible supply chains were able to adapt, reroute shipments, and maintain continuity. As a result, companies are now prioritizing supply chain redundancy, buffer stock strategies, and digital procurement solutions to ensure resilience in future crises.

Risk management in logistics also extends to compliance risks, regulatory changes, and environmental sustainability mandates. Governments are increasingly enforcing carbon emissions regulations, sustainability reporting requirements, and ethical labor laws that impact logistics operations. Non-compliance can result in hefty fines, trade restrictions, and reputational damage. To mitigate compliance risks, businesses must stay updated on regulatory changes, invest in sustainability initiatives, and implement governance frameworks that ensure alignment with global trade laws.

To manage risks effectively, logistics companies are integrating artificial intelligence and predictive analytics into their supply chain operations. AI-driven risk assessment tools analyze historical data, real-time market trends, and geopolitical events to forecast potential disruptions before they occur. Businesses use predictive analytics to identify weak links in supply chains, optimize contingency plans, and simulate crisis scenarios to test their response capabilities. The use of digital twins, virtual replicas of supply chain operations enables businesses to simulate disruptions, model alternative strategies, and refine decision-making processes in real time.

Another essential component of risk management is business continuity planning (BCP). Companies must develop comprehensive BCP frameworks that outline emergency response protocols, crisis communication strategies, and backup supply chain networks to ensure smooth operations during disruptions.

Businesses conduct regular risk assessments, supply chain audits, and scenario-based training drills to prepare for worst-case situations. Companies that prioritize risk management and crisis preparedness gain a competitive advantage by ensuring faster recovery, reduced losses, and sustained customer confidence during unforeseen events.

Insurance plays a key role in mitigating financial risks associated with logistics disruptions. Businesses invest in cargo insurance, trade credit insurance, cyber liability insurance, and business interruption insurance to protect against damages, financial losses, and supply chain liabilities. Insurance policies provide coverage for theft, shipment delays, damaged goods, cybersecurity breaches, and geopolitical risks, allowing businesses to recover losses and maintain stability during crises.

In a world where supply chain disruptions are inevitable, resilience, agility, and proactive risk management determine a company's ability to withstand and recover from challenges. Businesses that adopt real-time risk monitoring, diversified supply chain strategies, and digital crisis response tools will be better equipped to navigate the complexities of global logistics. The integration of AI-driven forecasting, blockchain security, and sustainability compliance will further strengthen supply chain resilience, ensuring long-term operational continuity and competitive advantage.

Artificial intelligence (AI) transforms how businesses identify, assess, and respond to logistics risks by providing predictive insights, real-time alerts, and automated decision-making capabilities. Traditional risk management strategies often relied on historical data, manual assessments, and reactive problem-solving, which limited the ability of businesses to respond swiftly to emerging threats. AI-powered risk management tools, on the other hand, use machine learning algorithms, data analytics, and pattern recognition to forecast potential disruptions before they occur, allowing companies to take proactive measures.

One of the most valuable applications of AI in logistics risk management is predictive analytics. AI-driven systems analyze historical supply chain data, weather conditions, geopolitical events, economic indicators, and transportation patterns to predict disruptions such as port congestion, supplier failures, shipment delays, and demand fluctuations. By leveraging AI-generated forecasts, logistics companies can adjust inventory levels, reroute shipments, and secure alternative suppliers to minimize potential losses.

AI-powered autonomous decision-making systems also play a crucial role in real-time risk response. In high-risk situations, such as severe weather conditions, strikes, or unexpected demand surges, AI-driven systems can automatically trigger contingency plans, allocate backup transportation, and recommend alternative logistics routes. These automated responses help businesses reduce human error, accelerate crisis resolution, and maintain operational continuity.

For instance, during the Suez Canal blockage in 2021, companies that used AI-based supply chain monitoring tools were able to predict shipment delays, reroute cargo through alternative ports, and adjust delivery schedules in real time, mitigating financial losses. AI-powered supply chain risk dashboards also provide logistics executives with instant visibility into potential disruptions, enabling faster and more informed decision-making.

Another critical AI-driven innovation is natural language processing (NLP), which allows businesses to monitor news reports, social media trends, and government advisories in real time to detect early warning signs of supply chain disruptions. For example, logistics companies can use NLP tools to track regulatory changes, labor union negotiations, and political developments that could impact global trade and logistics operations.

In an increasingly interconnected world, no business operates in isolation. Collaboration between supply chain stakeholders, manufacturers, suppliers, logistics providers, and customers—is essential for mitigating risks and ensuring resilience. A fragmented supply chain is more vulnerable to disruptions, miscommunication, and inefficiencies, while an integrated and well-coordinated network improves response times, adaptability, and risk-sharing.

Supply chain collaboration involves sharing data, coordinating contingency plans, and aligning risk management strategies across different entities. Businesses that work closely with freight forwarders, third-party logistics providers (3PLs), and customs authorities can anticipate potential disruptions earlier and develop joint crisis response plans. For example, companies in the automotive and electronics industries have established multi-supplier agreements to prevent production shutdowns caused by shortages of critical components such as semiconductors.

Building a resilient supply chain also requires businesses to adopt a multi-sourcing strategy rather than relying on a single supplier or geographic region. The COVID-19 pandemic exposed the vulnerabilities of over-concentrated supply chains, particularly in industries that relied heavily on Chinese manufacturing hubs. To mitigate such risks, companies are now diversifying their supplier base by sourcing from multiple regions, nearshoring production closer to key markets, and maintaining strategic safety stock levels.

Another critical component of resilience planning is dynamic inventory management. Businesses must strike a balance between lean inventory models that minimize holding costs and buffer stock strategies that provide extra capacity during crises. Advances in real-time inventory tracking and AI-driven demand forecasting have made it possible for companies to adjust stock levels dynamically, reducing the risks of overstocking or understocking during uncertain market conditions.

Collaboration between governments, regulatory bodies, and industry associations also plays a key role in developing standardized risk management frameworks, improving trade security protocols, and ensuring the smooth movement of goods across borders. Many governments have introduced supply chain continuity initiatives, disaster recovery programs, and public-private partnerships to enhance logistics resilience against global shocks.

As logistics operations become more digitized and complex, businesses must integrate advanced risk management technologies, build strong partnerships, and adopt flexible strategies to stay resilient in an unpredictable world. The future of risk management in logistics will be shaped by AI-driven automation, blockchain-enhanced supply chain transparency, IoT-enabled real-time monitoring, and predictive crisis modeling.

Companies that prioritize resilience, invest in smart technologies, and foster supply chain collaboration will not only mitigate risks but also gain a competitive edge by maintaining operational stability, reducing costs, and ensuring high levels of customer satisfaction. Businesses must transition from reactive crisis management to proactive risk mitigation strategies that enable them to predict disruptions, respond swiftly, and adapt to evolving global challenges.

7.1 Financial Risk Management in Logistics

Financial risks in logistics are among the most significant concerns for businesses, as currency fluctuations, fuel price volatility, tariff changes, and supplier bankruptcies can drastically affect operational costs. Without proper financial planning, companies may face budget overruns, reduced profit margins, and disrupted supply chains.

One of the primary financial risks in logistics is currency exchange rate volatility. Businesses that operate in global markets must deal with multiple currencies, and fluctuations in exchange rates can increase procurement costs, transportation expenses, and overall financial instability. Companies engaged in international trade often use foreign exchange (forex) hedging strategies, forward contracts, and currency diversification to reduce exposure to currency risk.

Fuel price fluctuations also pose a major financial risk in logistics, as transportation costs account for a significant portion of supply chain expenses. Companies that rely on long-haul trucking, ocean freight, or air cargo must closely monitor oil price trends and government policies on fuel taxation. To mitigate fuel-related risks, logistics providers implement fuel-efficient routing, invest in electric or hybrid transportation fleets, and negotiate long-term fuel contracts with suppliers.

Another financial risk stems from tariff changes and trade policy shifts. Countries frequently adjust import/export tariffs, impose sanctions, or introduce new trade agreements that impact logistics costs and supply chain planning. Businesses must stay updated on global trade regulations, develop flexible sourcing strategies, and leverage duty-free trade zones to minimize exposure to tariff risks.

Supplier bankruptcy and financial instability among logistics partners can also disrupt supply chains. If a manufacturer, shipping carrier, or third-party logistics provider (3PL) becomes financially insolvent, companies may struggle to find alternative suppliers or transport solutions on short notice. To prevent such risks, businesses must conduct financial risk assessments of key suppliers, maintain backup supplier agreements, and diversify logistics partnerships.

Cargo insurance and financial risk mitigation tools play a critical role in protecting businesses from losses due to damaged, delayed, or stolen shipments. Companies invest in comprehensive cargo insurance policies, trade credit insurance, and liability coverage to safeguard against financial losses from supply chain disruptions, natural disasters, and shipment delays.

7.2 The Role of Emergency Response Networks in Crisis Recovery

When a major supply chain disruption occurs, companies must activate emergency response networks to contain the impact and restore operations quickly. These networks include government agencies, logistics partners, crisis response teams, and technology-driven rapid response systems. Businesses that develop well-structured emergency response networks can minimize downtime, maintain customer service levels, and prevent significant financial losses.

Emergency response planning starts with business continuity plans (BCP) that outline step-by-step procedures for responding to disruptions. These plans must include alternative supplier agreements, backup transportation routes, contingency warehouse locations, and real-time crisis communication protocols. Regularly testing these plans through simulated crisis drills and scenario-based training exercises ensures that companies can react swiftly in actual emergencies.

Technology plays a crucial role in crisis recovery by providing real-time data visibility and automated risk alerts. Logistics companies use IoT sensors, AI-driven risk monitoring platforms, and blockchain-based shipment tracking to detect disruptions as they happen. For example, if a cargo ship carrying critical raw materials is delayed due to bad weather, automated logistics systems can reroute shipments, notify customers, and adjust inventory levels to minimize supply chain disruptions.

Public-private partnerships between governments, logistics firms, and humanitarian organizations are essential in responding to large-scale crises, such as natural disasters, geopolitical conflicts, and global pandemics. Many governments establish emergency supply chain task forces to ensure the uninterrupted flow of medical supplies, food, and essential goods during crises. Logistics providers work closely with these agencies to coordinate disaster relief logistics, transport essential goods efficiently, and rebuild supply chain infrastructure.

Another key aspect of emergency response networks is supplying chain redundancy. Businesses that depend on a single supply route or warehouse facility are more vulnerable to disruptions. By implementing multi-node distribution networks, regional fulfillment centers, and decentralized inventory systems, companies can ensure continued operations even if one part of the supply chain is impacted.

The crisis response also requires effective stakeholder communication. Logistics firms must have clear communication protocols with suppliers, carriers, customers, and regulatory authorities to ensure transparency during disruptions. Companies that provide real-time shipment updates, proactive risk alerts, and flexible rescheduling options build stronger relationships with customers and minimize reputational damage.

Risk management in logistics is about anticipating potential disruptions, preparing contingency plans, and leveraging technology to enhance response times. Financial risks such as currency fluctuations, fuel price volatility, and supplier insolvency require businesses to adopt forex hedging, diversified logistics strategies, and cargo insurance policies to minimize losses. The ability to activate emergency response networks, utilize AI-driven crisis forecasting, and establish supply chain redundancies ensures business continuity in times of disruption.

As logistics operations become increasingly digitized, companies that integrate predictive **analytics, blockchain security, and AI-powered crisis response tools** will gain a **competitive advantage by maintaining operational stability and customer trust.** Businesses must transition from a **reactive risk management approach to a proactive resilience-building strategy,** ensuring that they can withstand and recover from global supply chain challenges.

CHAPTER EIGHT

Customer Experience and Service Optimization in Logistics

Customer experience is becoming a key differentiator in logistics, as businesses recognize that fast, reliable, and transparent service is critical to gaining and retaining customers. In an era where e-commerce growth, on-demand deliveries, and real-time tracking shape consumer expectations, logistics providers must optimize their service models, invest in last-mile delivery solutions, and leverage digital technology to improve customer satisfaction. Companies that focus on service excellence, proactive problem resolution, and personalized delivery experiences build stronger relationships with customers and drive long-term business success.

The logistics industry was once focused primarily on cost efficiency and operational optimization, but today, customer experience has taken center stage. With the rise of platforms like Amazon, Alibaba, and Shopify, consumers expect same-day or next-day delivery, real-time shipment tracking, and seamless returns. Logistics providers must align their delivery speed, accuracy, and responsiveness with these evolving demands to remain competitive. A well-optimized logistics experience reduces delays, minimizes errors, enhances transparency, and increases customer trust.

Service optimization in logistics requires end-to-end visibility, smart logistics infrastructure, and a customer-centric approach to operations. The ability to provide real-time updates, flexible delivery options, and responsive customer support determines whether a business meets or exceeds customer expectations. Companies that fail to address service inefficiencies risk customer dissatisfaction, negative reviews, and lost revenue.

Last-mile delivery is one of the most critical and challenging aspects of logistics, as it directly impacts the customer's experience. The final leg of a shipment journey from a distribution center to the customer's doorstep—determines whether the delivery is on time, in good condition, and aligned with customer preferences. Businesses that optimize last-mile logistics can reduce costs, increase efficiency, and provide customers with greater convenience.

One of the biggest pain points in last-mile delivery is delays due to traffic congestion, inaccurate addresses, and inefficient routing. To solve these challenges, logistics companies are adopting AI-powered route optimization tools that analyze real-time traffic data, weather conditions, and road closures to select the most efficient delivery routes. Predictive analytics helps businesses anticipate delivery bottlenecks and adjust logistics schedules dynamically.

The use of micro-fulfillment centers and urban distribution hubs is also reshaping last-mile logistics. Instead of relying on centralized warehouses, companies are setting up regional fulfillment centers closer to high-demand areas, allowing for faster order processing and shorter delivery distances. This strategy is particularly effective for e-commerce retailers, grocery delivery services, and subscription-based businesses that require rapid delivery turnaround times.

The rise of alternative delivery methods, including drones, autonomous vehicles, and smart lockers, is further improving last-mile logistics. Companies like Amazon, Walmart, and FedEx are investing in autonomous delivery robots and self-driving vehicles that reduce dependency on human drivers and minimize delivery costs. Smart lockers provide a secure, contactless delivery option that allows customers to pick up packages at their convenience, reducing the risk of failed deliveries and package theft.

Flexibility in last-mile delivery is another key factor in service optimization. Customers now expect options such as scheduled delivery windows, delivery rescheduling, and alternative pickup locations. Companies that offer real-time delivery tracking, SMS/email notifications, and AI-powered chatbots for customer support enhance customer satisfaction by providing transparency and convenience.

Technology is playing a pivotal role in transforming logistics service quality, response times, and customer engagement. The integration of big data analytics, IoT-enabled shipment tracking, and AI-powered customer support systems ensures that logistics companies can anticipate customer needs, resolve issues proactively, and personalize the delivery experience.

Real-time tracking and predictive delivery insights are reshaping customer interactions with logistics services. Customers no longer want vague delivery estimates; they expect precise tracking information, proactive notifications, and real-time shipment updates. GPS tracking, IoT sensors, and AI-driven logistics platforms allow businesses to provide accurate ETAs, automatic delay alerts, and customized delivery status updates.

AI-driven customer support is enhancing logistics service responsiveness. AI-powered chatbots, virtual assistants, and voice-based customer service solutions enable businesses to handle customer inquiries 24/7, resolve common issues instantly, and streamline communication channels. Instead of waiting for a customer service representative, customers can use AI-driven self-service portals to track shipments, update delivery preferences, and initiate return requests.

Blockchain technology is also improving customer trust by enhancing transparency and security in logistics transactions. Blockchain-based supply chain solutions provide tamper-proof records of shipments, reduce fraud, and ensure accurate documentation of deliveries. Customers can verify the authenticity and origin of their shipments in real time, reducing disputes and increasing trust in the supply chain.

Reverse logistics, or the management of product returns, is another crucial aspect of customer experience. A seamless and hassle-free returns process improves customer satisfaction and encourages repeat purchases. Companies that implement automated return processing, AI-driven return authorization, and instant refund solutions enhance the overall shopping and delivery experience. Retailers that offer free and flexible return policies, along with self-service return drop-off points, gain a competitive advantage by simplifying post-purchase logistics for customers.

Customer expectations for sustainability and eco-friendly logistics solutions are also shaping service optimization strategies. Businesses are integrating carbon-neutral shipping options, electric delivery fleets, and biodegradable packaging materials to appeal to environmentally conscious consumers. Companies that adopt green logistics practices, optimize delivery routes to reduce fuel consumption, and offset carbon emissions are gaining favor with customers who prioritize sustainability.

Customer experience in logistics is no longer just about getting a package from point A to point B, it is about delivering convenience, transparency, and reliability. Companies that optimize their last-mile logistics, invest in AI-driven customer support, and provide real-time tracking solutions enhance customer loyalty and build long-term brand trust. The future of logistics will be hyper-personalized, automated, and sustainability-driven, with businesses leveraging AI, blockchain, and predictive analytics to continuously improve service quality.

As consumer expectations continue to evolve, logistics providers must stay ahead by offering flexible delivery options, ensuring seamless returns, and integrating sustainable practices. Companies that prioritize customer experience as a core component of their logistics strategy will gain a competitive advantage in an increasingly fast-paced, on-demand economy.

Customer experience in logistics has shifted from being a secondary concern to a competitive advantage as businesses recognize that speed, convenience, transparency, and flexibility directly impact consumer satisfaction. While we have explored the role of last-mile delivery and technology in service optimization, two additional areas require further discussion: the impact of personalization in logistics services and how businesses can use data analytics to predict and exceed customer expectations.

Personalization has become a key factor in customer experience, as consumers now expect services tailored to their unique needs. Logistics companies that offer customized delivery options, dynamic pricing, and flexible service models build stronger relationships with customers and increase long-term loyalty.

One of the most visible forms of personalization in logistics is customized delivery scheduling. Customers no longer want rigid delivery timeframes, they prefer to choose when, where, and how their shipments arrive. Businesses are responding by offering the same day, the next day, or scheduled delivery windows that fit the customer's lifestyle. Some companies even provide real-time rescheduling options, in-app delivery time selection, and evening or weekend delivery services to cater to busy professionals and urban dwellers.

Another growing trend in personalized logistics is preferred delivery locations. Instead of limiting deliveries to home or office addresses, companies are offering alternative pickup points, locker drop-offs, and even delivery to vehicle trunks for added convenience. Retailers like Amazon and Walmart have implemented "click and collect" models where customers can pick up their orders at designated locations, reducing missed deliveries and improving satisfaction.

Personalized packaging and presentation are also influencing customer perceptions of logistics services. Brands that ship products with premium, eco-friendly, or gift-ready packaging create a more memorable unboxing experience, enhancing customer loyalty. Some businesses allow customers to choose special gift wrapping, handwritten notes, or discreet packaging for sensitive products, further improving personalization.

Subscription-based logistics services are gaining traction, especially in e-commerce, meal kit deliveries, and fashion retail. Companies are offering subscription-based shipping models where customers can sign up for unlimited deliveries, priority shipping, or scheduled replenishment of essential items. For example, Amazon Prime members benefit from exclusive delivery perks, while grocery delivery services offer subscription-based weekly shipments of fresh produce.

Beyond physical delivery, logistics personalization is expanding into proactive customer service. AI-driven customer support tools analyze past customer interactions, anticipate issues, and provide proactive solutions before complaints arise. If a shipment delay is expected, customers receive automatic notifications with alternative options, compensation offers, or real-time tracking updates.

Data analytics is redefining logistics customer service by enabling businesses to analyze customer behavior, optimize delivery routes, and enhance operational efficiency. Companies that use big data, AI-driven insights, and predictive analytics can anticipate customer needs, prevent service failures, and deliver more efficient logistics solutions.

One of the most effective applications of data analytics in logistics is demand forecasting. By analyzing historical sales trends, seasonal demand patterns, and external factors such as economic conditions and social trends, businesses can predict which products will be in high demand, where the demand will be strongest, and how much inventory to stock. Retailers and logistics providers use predictive inventory management tools to ensure that they have the right products available in the right locations, reducing stockouts and overstocking.

Real-time data analytics also transforming route optimization and delivery performance. AI-powered logistics platforms analyze traffic patterns, weather conditions, and delivery time variability to select the fastest and most efficient routes. This level of optimization reduces fuel costs, minimizes delays, and improves on-time delivery rates. Businesses that leverage AI-driven logistics solutions gain a significant competitive advantage by shortening delivery windows and enhancing customer satisfaction.

Customer sentiment analysis is another way businesses use data analytics to improve service quality. AI-powered tools scan social media, online reviews, and customer feedback platforms to identify trends in consumer complaints, preferences, and emerging expectations. If a logistics provider notices a rise in negative sentiment about delayed shipments or damaged goods, it can take proactive steps to improve warehouse handling, increase communication transparency, or adjust carrier partnerships.

Predictive maintenance is revolutionizing logistics fleet management, ensuring that vehicles remain in optimal working condition to prevent unexpected breakdowns. IoT-enabled sensors installed in delivery trucks continuously monitor engine health, fuel efficiency, and tire conditions, allowing businesses to schedule maintenance before mechanical failures occur. This reduces downtime, improves delivery reliability, and lowers maintenance costs.

AI-driven chatbots and customer service assistants are also playing a role in enhancing the customer experience. These smart systems can answer queries instantly, provide shipment status updates, assist with delivery changes, and even handle complaints autonomously. By automating customer interactions, businesses improve response times and customer satisfaction rates.

Another transformative application of data analytics is personalized pricing models. Some logistics providers are implementing dynamic pricing strategies where shipping costs fluctuate based on demand, delivery urgency, and customer loyalty status. Customers who frequently use premium logistics services or subscribe to membership-based shipping programs can receive discounted or preferential pricing.

Data-driven insights are also improving reverse logistics and return management. Businesses analyze return patterns to identify high-return products, detect fraudulent return behaviors, and optimize refund processing times. Companies that streamline their return policies and offer instant refunds, drop-off return locations, and hassle-free exchanges increase customer trust and retention.

8.1 The Psychological Impact of Logistics Service Quality on Customer Loyalty

Customer satisfaction in logistics is deeply influenced by emotional and psychological factors, not just the physical movement of goods. A well-executed delivery builds trust and strengthens brand loyalty, while a failed or delayed shipment creates frustration, negative reviews, and even long-term brand abandonment.

One of the most critical psychological aspects of logistics service is expectation management. Customers are more forgiving of delays when companies proactively communicate issues, offer real-time updates, and provide alternatives. However, uncertainty, lack of communication, and missed deadlines erode customer confidence. Companies that use automated alerts, real-time tracking, and proactive customer support maintain high customer satisfaction levels, even in cases of unforeseen delays.

The speed and reliability of delivery also shape customer purchase behavior and repeat business rates. Consumers who experience smooth, hassle-free deliveries are more likely to make repeat purchases and recommend the brand to others. On the other hand, a single bad logistics experience can drive a customer to switch brands or platforms. This is why companies invest in data-driven last-mile logistics, AI-powered delivery forecasts, and flexible shipping options to maintain service consistency.

The emotional impact of uncertainty on delivery is particularly high in industries where shipments carry significant personal or business value. For example, customers expecting urgent medical supplies, high-value electronics, or perishable goods feel heightened anxiety when delivery accuracy is compromised.

Logistics companies that prioritize fast response times, high shipment visibility, and contingency solutions not only reduce customer stress but also build a reputation for reliability.

Another psychological factor affecting customer loyalty is the perception of effort. Customers who have to call customer service multiple times, follow up on delays, or go through complicated return processes perceive the logistics experience as stressful and inconvenient. Companies that provide one-click return options, chatbot-assisted issue resolution, and hassle-free refund processing reduce customer effort, leading to higher satisfaction and retention rates.

Logistics also plays a role in brand differentiation. A seamless delivery process enhances the brand image, particularly in industries where customers associate fast and reliable shipping with product quality. Luxury brands, for instance, invest in high-end, personalized delivery experiences, including premium packaging, white-glove delivery services, and direct communication with delivery agents. This level of personalization reinforces brand identity and fosters long-term customer relationships.

8.2 The Role of Sustainability in Enhancing the Customer Experience

Sustainability in logistics is no longer just an ethical choice—it is becoming a key driver of customer preference and brand loyalty. Consumers are increasingly aware of the environmental impact of supply chains and are choosing brands that prioritize eco-friendly shipping, sustainable packaging, and carbon-neutral delivery models.

One of the most visible aspects of sustainable logistics is green last-mile delivery. Companies are investing in electric delivery vehicles, bicycle couriers, and eco-friendly routing algorithms to reduce carbon emissions in urban logistics. Brands that offer "green delivery" options at checkout allow customers to actively participate in sustainability efforts, fostering a sense of shared responsibility.

Sustainable packaging is another factor shaping customer perception of logistics services. Many consumers prefer minimalist, recyclable, or biodegradable packaging over excessive plastic wrapping and wasteful materials. Companies that use compostable packaging, reusable mailers, or package-free shipping options create a positive emotional response, reinforcing brand loyalty.

The concept of "slow logistics" is emerging as a customer-driven sustainability trend. While fast shipping remains a priority, many customers are now willing to wait longer for deliveries if it means reducing the environmental impact. Some e-commerce platforms allow customers to select "eco-friendly shipping" options that consolidate orders to minimize carbon footprint. Logistics providers that educate customers about the benefits of slower, more sustainable shipping models can enhance their brand reputation while reducing operational costs.

Blockchain technology is also improving supply chain transparency, allowing customers to verify ethical sourcing, fair labor practices, and carbon impact metrics in logistics operations. Companies that integrate blockchain-enabled sustainability tracking into their customer interfaces build trust and credibility with eco-conscious consumers.

Another sustainability trend influencing customer experience is circular logistics, which focuses on reducing waste and promoting product lifecycle sustainability. Businesses are adopting reverse logistics models that encourage repairs, refurbishments, and second-hand resale options. For example, fashion brands offering take-back programs for used clothing or electronics companies providing refurbished device trade-ins create an engaging, customer-centric approach to sustainability.

CHAPTER NINE

Global Trade and Supply Chain Expansion

The expansion of global trade has transformed logistics into a highly interconnected and dynamic industry, enabling businesses to source materials, manufacture products, and distribute goods across international markets. As companies scale their operations beyond domestic borders, they must navigate complex trade regulations, geopolitical uncertainties, currency fluctuations, and evolving consumer demands. Success in global logistics requires businesses to develop scalable supply chain models, optimize cross-border transportation networks, and build strong partnerships with international trade stakeholders.

The global supply chain landscape is shaped by technological advancements, free trade agreements, regulatory shifts, and sustainability trends. Businesses that strategically position distribution centers, leverage digital trade platforms, and comply with international trade laws gain a competitive advantage in reaching new markets efficiently. However, companies that fail to plan for customs regulations, trade tariffs, and global disruptions risk facing costly delays, shipment losses, and reputational damage.

To thrive in global logistics, businesses must develop agile, resilient, and technology-driven supply chains that can withstand challenges such as port congestion, supply shortages, inflation, and geopolitical tensions. With supply chain networks expanding across multiple continents, time zones, and regulatory environments, businesses must balance cost efficiency, service reliability, and compliance with international trade laws.

One of the biggest challenges in global logistics is navigating trade regulations, customs procedures, and cross-border compliance requirements. Every country has its own set of import/export laws, tariff classifications, and documentation processes, making it critical for businesses to stay informed and ensure regulatory compliance.

Customs clearance delays are among the most common pain points in international trade. Businesses that fail to provide accurate shipping documentation, correct product classifications, and compliance with import restrictions risk longer transit times, additional costs, and shipment seizures. To prevent these issues, companies rely on customs brokers, automated trade compliance platforms, and AI-driven classification systems that ensure smooth border crossings.

The Harmonized System (HS) code classification is a globally recognized system for categorizing goods in trade. Assigning the correct HS code to products determines applicable tariffs, import duties, and trade restrictions. Misclassification can lead to fines, increased taxes, or customs clearance delays. Many companies use automated HS code classification tools to ensure accuracy in trade declarations.

Trade agreements play a crucial role in facilitating global supply chain expansion. Businesses that leverage free trade agreements (FTAs), preferential trade zones, and customs unions can reduce costs and improve efficiency. For example, the African Continental Free Trade Area (AfCFTA), the United States-Mexico-Canada Agreement (USMCA), and the European Union Customs Union provide trade benefits such as tariff reductions, simplified customs procedures, and faster market access. Companies that align their logistics strategies with these trade agreements gain cost advantages and operational flexibility.

In addition to customs compliance, businesses must also adhere to sanctions laws, export control regulations, and embargo restrictions. Governments impose trade sanctions on specific countries, industries, or individuals, affecting global logistics operations. Companies must conduct sanctions screening and regulatory due diligence to ensure that their supply chain partners are not involved in restricted or illegal trade activities.

Expanding into international markets requires businesses to optimize cross-border transportation and distribution networks to ensure cost efficiency, timely deliveries, and seamless customer experiences. Selecting the right transportation mode, warehouse locations, and distribution strategies is critical for achieving global scalability and operational flexibility.

Another key aspect of global logistics expansion is strategic warehousing and regional distribution centers. Businesses must position warehouses in strategic trade hubs that allow for quick inventory replenishment, reduced shipping costs, and shorter delivery times. Many companies are expanding their fulfillment networks in key logistics hubs such as Singapore, Dubai, Rotterdam, and Mexico City to ensure fast and efficient global distribution.

The rise in cross-border e-commerce has also increased the demand for direct-to-consumer (DTC) international shipping solutions. Companies that sell products internationally must integrate localized logistics infrastructure, customs-friendly shipping policies, and international returns management to enhance the cross-border customer experience.

Global supply chains are increasingly leveraging technology-driven logistics platforms that automate cross-border tracking, customs documentation, and compliance verification. AI-powered logistics platforms optimize shipping routes, reduce transit delays, and enhance shipment visibility by providing real-time tracking updates across multiple jurisdictions.

Technology also plays a key role in automating trade finance and payment processing in global logistics. Many businesses struggle with currency exchange risks, delayed international payments, and complex invoicing requirements. Blockchain-based smart contracts and digital trade finance platforms streamline international transactions, reducing fraud risks, currency fluctuations, and payment delays.

The future of global logistics will be shaped by trade digitalization, automation, and geopolitical shifts. Businesses that embrace AI-driven logistics solutions, blockchain-based trade documentation, and cloud-based global supply chain platforms will gain a competitive edge in navigating complex international trade environments.

Sustainability will also play an increasingly significant role in cross-border logistics. Governments worldwide are implementing carbon taxes, emission reduction mandates, and eco-friendly trade policies that impact global supply chain operations. Businesses that invest in sustainable logistics solutions, green transportation technologies, and circular supply chain models will improve compliance with environmental regulations and meet evolving consumer expectations.

With global trade dynamics evolving rapidly, businesses must remain agile, resilient, and proactive in expanding their supply chain networks. Companies that build strong international trade partnerships, invest in digital logistics infrastructure, and optimize cross-border distribution models will be well-positioned for long-term success in global markets.

Expanding into global markets presents both opportunities and challenges for businesses looking to scale their logistics operations. Companies must navigate regulatory complexities, customs procedures, and supply chain disruptions while optimizing transportation, warehousing, and distribution networks for maximum efficiency and cost savings.

By leveraging free trade agreements, AI-driven trade compliance tools, and multimodal logistics solutions, businesses can streamline international shipping, reduce transit delays, and enhance cross-border supply chain visibility. Companies that proactively manage global trade risks, invest in digital trade platforms, and align their logistics strategies with sustainability goals will maintain a competitive edge in international markets.

Global trade does not operate in isolation, it is shaped by geopolitical shifts, economic policies, and international trade relationships. Businesses expanding into global markets must be aware of trade wars, political instability, sanctions, currency fluctuations, and regional conflicts that could impact supply chain efficiency.

Trade wars and tariffs have become a defining factor in global logistics, affecting import/export costs, sourcing decisions, and supply chain realignments. The U.S.-China trade war, for example, led to higher tariffs on Chinese goods, forcing businesses to diversify sourcing strategies and explore alternative manufacturing locations in Vietnam, India, and Mexico. Similarly, the uncertainty surrounding Brexit disrupted European supply chains, requiring businesses to adjust customs procedures, revise trade contracts, and navigate new compliance requirements.

Sanctions and embargoes also influence global trade expansion. Countries facing economic sanctions may experience trade restrictions that impact logistics operations, banking transactions, and shipping routes. Businesses must conduct due diligence on international trade partners to ensure compliance with sanctions regulations and avoid legal penalties. Many logistics providers use automated sanctions screening tools and trade compliance software to verify whether shipments or business dealings involve restricted countries, individuals, or entities.

Political instability and regional conflicts can create unexpected supply chain disruptions, port closures, and regulatory changes. For example, conflicts in Eastern Europe, the Middle East, and Africa have affected transportation corridors, delayed cargo shipments, and increased security concerns for logistics providers. Businesses operating in politically unstable regions must develop contingency plans, establish alternative supply routes, and invest in risk management solutions to mitigate potential disruptions.

Currency fluctuations and inflation directly impact global trade costs. A strong or weak currency affects the cost of imports, export competitiveness, and supply chain financing. Companies engaged in cross-border logistics often use hedging strategies, multi-currency invoicing, and trade finance solutions to manage exchange rate volatility and stabilize international transactions. Digital trade platforms are increasingly integrating blockchain-based smart contracts and digital payment solutions to reduce the risks associated with currency fluctuations.

As global trade becomes more complex, businesses are turning to digital supply chain ecosystems to enhance efficiency, transparency, and resilience in international logistics. Digital ecosystems bring together manufacturers, suppliers, freight forwarders, customs authorities, and distribution networks on a single, integrated platform, streamlining trade processes and reducing operational inefficiencies.

One of the most transformative advancements in global logistics is blockchain-based supply chain visibility. Blockchain technology enables businesses to create tamper-proof, real-time records of transactions, shipment movements, and compliance documentation. Companies that use blockchain for trade documentation, smart contracts, and customs processing reduce paperwork, minimize fraud risks, and speed up cross-border trade. For example, Maersk and IBM's TradeLens platform digitized global shipping transactions, significantly improving supply chain transparency and efficiency.

AI-powered logistics management systems are also playing a crucial role in international supply chain optimization. AI-driven platforms analyze real-time shipping data, demand patterns, and economic trends to provide businesses with predictive insights on trade disruptions, cost fluctuations, and optimal shipping routes. By leveraging AI, businesses can automate decision-making, optimize inventory levels, and proactively adjust logistics strategies to align with market demands.

The Internet of Things (IoT) enhancing cross-border logistics by enabling real-time shipment tracking, predictive maintenance for fleet vehicles, and automated inventory management. IoT sensors monitor cargo temperature, humidity levels, and transit conditions in industries such as pharmaceuticals, food, and high-value electronics, ensuring that shipments meet international quality and compliance standards.

Cloud-based digital supply chain platforms are improving collaboration between international trade partners, allowing businesses to manage customs documentation, invoicing, compliance checks, and logistics tracking in real time. Companies using cloud logistics solutions experience faster customs clearance, fewer trade disputes, and improved supply chain agility.

E-commerce globalization is further driving the need for seamless cross-border logistics solutions. Companies selling to international consumers must offer localized logistics services, duty-inclusive shipping options, and multi-currency payment systems to simplify the buying experience. Businesses that integrate cross-border e-commerce platforms, regional fulfillment centers, and international last-mile delivery networks gain an advantage in expanding global reach and improving customer satisfaction.

Digital freight marketplaces are emerging as a solution for global shipping optimization, connecting shippers with freight carriers in real time. Platforms like Flexport, Freightos, and Convoy are revolutionizing freight booking, dynamic pricing, and real-time shipment tracking, reducing logistics costs and improving operational visibility.

9.1 The Impact of Sustainability on Global Trade and Supply Chains

Sustainability has become a critical component of global trade and logistics strategy as businesses, governments, and consumers demand greener supply chain operations. Companies that fail to integrate sustainable logistics practices face increasing pressure from regulatory bodies, environmental organizations, and market competitors. As a result, sustainability is now a strategic priority for businesses expanding into international markets.

One of the most pressing sustainability challenges in global logistics is reducing carbon emissions from transportation. The logistics industry is responsible for a significant percentage of global greenhouse gas (GHG) emissions, particularly from ocean freight, air cargo, and road transportation. To address this, businesses are investing in alternative fuels, electric delivery fleets, and carbon offset programs. Shipping companies are shifting toward liquefied natural gas (LNG)-powered vessels, hydrogen fuel cells, and wind-assisted propulsion systems to minimize environmental impact.

In many regions, governments have introduced strict carbon regulations and sustainability reporting requirements that affect cross-border logistics. The European Union's Carbon Border Adjustment Mechanism (CBAM) imposes taxes on carbon-intensive imports, forcing businesses to reassess sourcing strategies and invest in low-emission logistics solutions. Similarly, new regulations such as the International Maritime Organization (IMO) 2023 emissions cap require shipping companies to improve fuel efficiency and adopt sustainable fleet management practices.

Another major sustainability factor in global trade is waste reduction and circular supply chains. Businesses are moving toward zero-waste logistics models, closed-loop supply chains, and sustainable packaging solutions to reduce the environmental footprint of international shipping. Many global brands now implement recyclable packaging, biodegradable shipping materials, and eco-friendly pallet designs to align sustainability commitments.

The push for green trade agreements is also shaping the future of global logistics. Governments are negotiating trade agreements that prioritize sustainability, renewable energy investments, and green supply chain innovations. For example, initiatives like the Green Freight Program and Climate Smart Trade policies incentivize businesses to adopt eco-friendly logistics strategies, such as carbon-neutral shipping and sustainable sourcing.

As sustainability becomes a non-negotiable aspect of global trade, businesses must align their logistics operations with environmental, social, and governance (ESG) standards to maintain compliance, attract investment, and meet consumer expectations. Companies that integrate sustainability metrics, carbon tracking software, and ethical sourcing strategies into their logistics frameworks will gain a competitive advantage in the evolving global supply chain landscape.

9.2 The Challenges of Talent Management in International Logistics

Expanding logistics operations into new international markets presents businesses with workforce challenges, cultural differences, and skills shortages. The success of global supply chains depends on talented logistics professionals, warehouse managers, customs brokers, and transportation specialists who understand the complexities of international trade.

One of the biggest challenges in talent management for global logistics is recruiting and retaining skilled workers in multiple regions. Many countries face labor shortages in key logistics roles, particularly in warehousing, freight handling, and supply chain analytics. The growing demand for AI-driven logistics, digital freight management, and automated warehousing has created a skills gap where companies struggle to find trained professionals capable of operating advanced logistics technologies.

Cultural differences and workforce diversity add another layer of complexity to international logistics management. Businesses operating across multiple countries and time zones must navigate language barriers, labor laws, and cultural expectations when managing supply chain teams. Successful companies invest in cross-cultural training programs, multilingual logistics platforms, and region-specific HR policies to foster collaboration and efficiency.

Logistics labor laws and workforce regulations vary significantly across different regions. Companies must ensure compliance with minimum wage laws, working hour restrictions, employee benefits, and safety regulations in each country where they operate. Non-compliance can lead to legal penalties, supply chain disruptions, and reputational damage. Businesses expanding globally must work closely with local HR specialists, labor law consultants, and government agencies to ensure they meet workforce regulations while maintaining productivity.

The rise of remote logistics management has changed how businesses handle international supply chain operations. Many companies now use cloud-based logistics software, AI-driven workforce analytics, and remote training platforms to coordinate global logistics teams from different locations. Virtual freight management systems allow logistics professionals to monitor shipments, track inventory, and optimize supply chain efficiency without being physically present at distribution centers.

To overcome talent shortages, businesses are investing in workforce automation, robotics, and AI-driven logistics assistants to fill labor gaps. Autonomous material handling robots, AI-powered warehouse management systems, and machine learning-driven supply chain optimization tools are reducing the dependency on manual labor while enhancing logistics efficiency.

Training and skill development are critical for building a globally competent logistics workforce. Companies expanding into new markets must invest in supply chain education, technical training, and leadership development programs to equip employees with the skills needed to navigate modern logistics challenges. Businesses that adopt continuous learning models, industry certifications, and mentorship programs will create highly skilled, adaptable logistics teams capable of handling international operations.

CHAPTER TEN

The Future of Logistics and Emerging Industry Trends

The logistics industry is undergoing a technological revolution, driven by advancements in automation, artificial intelligence (AI), digital supply chain networks, and sustainability-focused innovations. As global supply chains become more interconnected, logistics providers must adopt next-generation technologies, predictive analytics, and agile business models to remain competitive. The future of logistics will be defined by autonomous transportation, AI-powered decision-making, blockchain transparency, and green logistics solutions that enhance efficiency, reduce costs, and improve sustainability.

With e-commerce growth, shifting consumer expectations, and regulatory changes, businesses must prepare for a more digital, data-driven, and automated logistics landscape. Logistics providers that leverage AI-driven analytics, invest in smart logistics platforms, and implement sustainable freight solutions will lead the industry in innovation, resilience, and profitability.

Autonomous logistics is set to reshape transportation, warehousing, and supply chain operations by reducing human dependency and increasing operational efficiency. AI-driven technologies are making it possible for businesses to automate supply chain decision-making, optimize fleet management, and enhance warehouse productivity with minimal human intervention.

One of the most significant advancements in logistics automation is self-driving freight transportation. Companies such as Tesla, Waymo, and Embark are pioneering autonomous trucks that use AI, LiDAR sensors, and GPS navigation to transport goods with greater precision and safety. Self-driving trucks reduce labor costs, eliminate human error, and enable 24/7 freight movement, improving delivery speeds and lowering transportation expenses.

Autonomous drones are also set to revolutionize last-mile delivery, particularly in urban and remote areas. Companies like Amazon, UPS, and Zipline are developing AI-powered drone delivery systems capable of navigating complex city landscapes, reducing delivery times, and enhancing service reliability. Drones offer a cost-effective, zero-emission alternative to traditional delivery vehicles, making them ideal for businesses looking to lower logistics costs and improve environmental sustainability.

In warehousing, robotic automation transforms inventory management, picking, and sorting operations. AI-powered robotic systems streamline warehouse workflows, reduce errors, and increase productivity. Companies such as Ocado, DHL, and Amazon have already implemented fully automated fulfillment centers where robots handle everything from inventory storage to order processing.

AI-powered decision-making is another game-changer in logistics. AI-driven predictive analytics enable companies to forecast demand fluctuations, detect supply chain bottlenecks, and dynamically adjust shipping routes in real-time. Machine learning algorithms analyze historical data, weather conditions, traffic congestion, and port delays to optimize logistics operations before disruptions occur.

Blockchain technology is revolutionizing logistics by providing tamper-proof, decentralized record-keeping that enhances supply chain transparency, security, and traceability. Traditional supply chains rely on manual documentation and fragmented data systems, which can lead to fraud, inefficiencies, and compliance issues. Blockchain eliminates these challenges by digitizing trade records, automating customs clearance, and securing global transactions.

One of the most promising applications of blockchain in logistics is smart contracts. These self-executing digital agreements automate payment processing, shipment tracking, and regulatory compliance, reducing delays and minimizing human intervention. Companies such as Maersk, IBM, and FedEx are implementing blockchain-powered logistics solutions to track shipments in real-time, authenticate product origins, and prevent counterfeiting.

Blockchain also improves supply chain traceability, particularly in industries where product authenticity, ethical sourcing, and regulatory compliance are crucial. The pharmaceutical, food, and luxury goods industries use blockchain to verify supply chain integrity, ensure quality control, and track product movement across international markets.

Sustainability is becoming a core pillar of logistics innovation, with businesses adopting eco-friendly freight solutions, carbon reduction strategies, and circular supply chain models to meet growing regulatory and consumer demands. Logistics providers that fail to implement green initiatives risk falling behind in an industry moving toward carbon neutrality.

One of the biggest trends in green logistics is the electrification of transportation fleets. Logistics companies are investing in electric trucks, hydrogen-powered freight vehicles, and alternative fuel solutions to lower carbon emissions and comply with global climate targets. Companies like Daimler, Volvo, and Nikola Motors are developing long-range electric freight trucks designed to replace diesel-powered vehicles in long-haul transportation.

Another major shift in sustainable logistics is the adoption of eco-friendly warehousing. Businesses are building solar-powered, energy-efficient distribution centers that use AI-driven climate control systems and sustainable building materials to minimize their environmental impact. Many companies are also implementing waste reduction programs, recyclable packaging, and carbon offset strategies to enhance their sustainability credentials.

Green last-mile delivery solutions are becoming more popular as cities enforce low-emission zones and urban congestion restrictions. Logistics companies are turning to electric delivery vans, bike couriers, and micro-fulfillment centers to reduce traffic congestion and carbon footprints in urban areas. Some companies even offer "carbon-neutral shipping" options, allowing customers to choose sustainable delivery methods at checkout.

Customer experience in logistics is evolving from standardized shipping models to hyper-personalized delivery solutions. As consumers demand more control, transparency, and flexibility, logistics providers must tailor their services to meet individual customer preferences.

One of the key innovations in customer-centric logistics is real-time adaptive delivery. AI-driven logistics platforms analyze customer location, preferred delivery times, and order history to create dynamic delivery schedules that align with consumer needs. Businesses that offer predictive ETAs, live tracking, and AI-powered delivery notifications significantly improve customer satisfaction and engagement.

Subscription-based logistics models are also gaining traction. Companies are introducing "frequent shopper" shipping memberships, on-demand delivery subscriptions, and scheduled replenishment programs that ensure seamless order fulfillment. These models create brand loyalty, improve retention rates, and enhance logistics efficiency.

The integration of augmented reality (AR) and virtual reality (VR) in logistics is another exciting development. AR-powered smart glasses assist warehouse workers in picking and sorting inventory, while VR-driven logistics simulations help businesses optimize warehouse layouts, train staff remotely, and test new supply chain strategies.

The future of logistics is being shaped by automation, AI-driven optimization, blockchain security, and sustainability. Businesses that adopt autonomous transportation, digital supply chain networks, and AI-powered logistics platforms will gain a competitive advantage in the rapidly evolving industry.

Sustainability will play a central role in future logistics strategies, with companies embracing green transportation solutions, energy-efficient warehousing, and eco-friendly supply chain initiatives to meet regulatory requirements and consumer expectations.

Customer experience will continue to be a driving force in logistics innovation, pushing companies to offer personalized delivery options, real-time tracking, and predictive shipping solutions that align with modern consumer demands.

The logistics industry is undergoing a fundamental transformation, driven by technological breakthroughs, evolving consumer expectations, and global economic shifts. As businesses strive to remain competitive in an increasingly complex supply chain landscape, they must adapt to automation, digitalization, sustainability, and geopolitical uncertainties. While we have explored autonomous logistics, blockchain, and green supply chains, two additional areas require further discussion: the impact of predictive logistics and AI-driven demand forecasting, and the evolution of global trade corridors and new supply chain strategies.

The future of logistics will be shaped by predictive analytics, artificial intelligence (AI), and real-time data monitoring, enabling businesses to anticipate disruptions, optimize inventory management, and enhance delivery precision. Traditional logistics models were largely reactive, relying on historical data and manual forecasting. However, modern supply chains are becoming proactive, leveraging AI-powered insights to make real-time decisions and reduce inefficiencies.

One of the most significant advancements in predictive logistics is AI-driven demand forecasting. Companies are integrating machine learning algorithms, big data analytics, and IoT sensors to predict future consumer demand, market trends, and supply chain risks. AI-driven demand forecasting helps businesses align inventory levels with market fluctuations, reduce stock shortages, and prevent overstocking, leading to lower operational costs and improved efficiency.

AI-powered supply chain monitoring platforms collect data from historical sales records, market trends, weather conditions, economic indicators, and consumer behavior patterns to create highly accurate demand projections. Companies that leverage predictive logistics tools can respond faster to unexpected demand surges, mitigate supply chain bottlenecks, and enhance production planning.

Another critical area where predictive analytics is transforming logistics is shipment tracking and delay prediction. Logistics providers use real-time GPS data, AI-powered traffic analysis, and weather forecasting tools to anticipate potential delays and automatically adjust delivery routes. This innovation helps businesses maintain delivery commitments, optimize fleet management, and improve customer satisfaction.

For instance, global shipping companies are integrating AI-powered predictive maintenance systems into their fleets, using real-time sensor data to detect potential mechanical failures before they happen. This technology reduces downtime, lowers repair costs, and improves fleet reliability, ensuring uninterrupted supply chain operations.

AI-driven automation is also being applied to warehouse management. Smart warehouses now feature self-learning robotic systems that analyze demand forecasts and automatically adjust inventory storage and replenishment cycles. By using AI to predict seasonal demand patterns, businesses can optimize warehouse space, reduce waste, and ensure that the right products are available at the right time.

Global trade corridors are shifting, reshaping supply chain networks and logistics strategies. As geopolitical tensions, climate change, and infrastructure investments alter traditional trade routes, businesses must adapt their supply chain models to emerging trade corridors and alternative shipping pathways.

One of the most significant trade developments in recent years is the China's Belt and Road Initiative (BRI), which is reshaping global supply chains by creating new rail, road, and maritime trade routes across Asia, Europe, and Africa. The expansion of rail freight between China and Europe has provided a faster, more cost-effective alternative to ocean shipping, reducing transit times and improving connectivity.

Similarly, the Northern Sea Route (NSR), made possible by Arctic ice melt, is emerging as a new shipping alternative for global freight transportation. The NSR significantly reduces transit times between Asia and Europe compared to traditional routes via the Suez Canal. As climate change continues to alter global trade routes, businesses must evaluate the risks and opportunities of shifting supply chains through newly accessible regions.

Another major trend shaping global logistics is the diversification of supply chain sourcing. The COVID-19 pandemic exposed the vulnerabilities of single-source supply chains, particularly those dependent on China. In response, businesses are adopting multi-sourcing strategies, investing in nearshoring, and expanding manufacturing hubs across Southeast Asia, Latin America, and Africa to reduce dependency on a single country or region.

Nearshoring, the practice of relocating manufacturing and distribution centers closer to key markets, is gaining traction as companies seek to reduce lead times, improve supply chain resilience, and lower transportation costs. Countries such as Mexico, India, and Vietnam are becoming attractive alternatives to China for manufacturing, as businesses seek greater supply chain agility.

Businesses are also reevaluating port congestion and trade route dependencies. The disruptions caused by the Suez Canal blockage and West Coast port congestion in the United States have prompted companies to diversify shipping routes, invest in secondary ports, and explore air freight alternatives for high-value goods.

The expansion of free trade agreements (FTAs) and regional trade blocs is another factor shaping the future of logistics. Agreements such as the African Continental Free Trade Area (AfCFTA), the Comprehensive and Progressive Agreement for Trans-Pacific Partnership (CPTPP), and the United States-Mexico-Canada Agreement (USMCA) are reducing trade barriers, lowering tariffs, and creating new opportunities for cross-border logistics optimization.

As automation and AI transform logistics, the future workforce will need to adapt to new technologies, roles, and skill sets. The logistics industry is shifting from labor-intensive operations to knowledge-based roles that require expertise in AI, data analytics, and supply chain optimization.

One of the biggest challenges facing the logistics industry is the shortage of skilled professionals capable of managing AI-powered logistics platforms, autonomous vehicles, and robotic warehouse systems. Businesses are investing in reskilling and upskilling programs to train employees in automation management, predictive analytics, and digital logistics solutions.

The rise of human-machine collaboration is changing how logistics teams operate. Rather than replacing human workers, automation is enhancing productivity by allowing humans to focus on complex decision-making, strategy, and customer service. Warehouses that deploy AI-driven robotic assistants improve order accuracy, reducing repetitive tasks, and creating a more efficient work environment.

In transportation, remote fleet monitoring and AI-driven logistics management platforms enabling logistics professionals to oversee multiple fleets, predict maintenance needs, and optimize fuel efficiency without being physically present at distribution centers.

As AI and automation reshape logistics roles, companies must develop workforce training programs, implement digital learning platforms, and foster a culture of technological adaptability to prepare employees for the next generation of supply chain management.

The future of logistics is being rewritten by automation, AI-driven decision-making, predictive analytics, and global trade realignments. Businesses that embrace digital transformation, invest in green supply chain initiatives, and adapt to evolving trade corridors will gain a competitive advantage in the fast-changing logistics landscape.

Predictive logistics and AI-powered demand forecasting are redefining inventory management, shipment tracking, and last-mile delivery, while autonomous transportation, blockchain transparency, and sustainable freight solutions are setting new industry standards.

10.1 The Rise of Hyper-Connected Supply Chains

Hyper-connected supply chains are the next step in logistics evolution, where AI, IoT, blockchain, and 5G connectivity create a fully integrated, real-time, and autonomous logistics ecosystem. Traditional supply chains relied on fragmented data, manual reporting, and siloed decision-making, leading to inefficiencies, delays, and miscommunication. Hyper-connected logistics networks eliminate these pain points by seamlessly integrating supply chain stakeholders, real-time analytics, and digital collaboration tools.

One of the biggest drivers of hyper-connectivity in logistics is the Internet of Things (IoT). IoT-enabled logistics systems use smart sensors, GPS tracking, RFID tags, and AI-powered monitoring tools to track shipments, monitor warehouse conditions, and optimize fleet management in real time. These technologies improve supply chain visibility, reduce lost shipments, and enhance inventory accuracy.

For example, IoT sensors in cold chain logistics monitor temperature, humidity, and storage conditions for perishable goods such as vaccines, fresh food, and pharmaceuticals. If temperature deviations occur during transit, AI-driven automation can adjust refrigeration settings, reroute shipments, or trigger real-time alerts to logistics teams, preventing spoilage and ensuring regulatory compliance.

Another significant aspect of hyper-connected supply chains is 5G-powered logistics networks. The integration of 5G technology into logistics enables ultra-fast data exchange, low-latency communication, and real-time coordination between warehouses, distribution centers, and transportation fleets. Logistics providers that adopt 5G connectivity can automate warehouse operations, implement smart traffic routing, and enhance fleet-to-fleet communication for seamless, real-time logistics management.

Blockchain technology plays a crucial role in securing hyper-connected supply chains. Blockchain-powered logistics systems eliminate fraudulent transactions, enhance contract transparency, and automate customs documentation processing through smart contracts. With blockchain-based track-and-trace solutions, companies can verify product authenticity, reduce counterfeiting risks, and improve trust between suppliers and customers.

The development of fully autonomous supply chains is also gaining momentum. Companies are implementing self-learning logistics platforms, AI-driven freight coordination, and automated supply chain decision-making tools that require minimal human intervention. These systems analyze historical trends, detect potential disruptions, and adjust shipping schedules dynamically to improve efficiency and cost savings.

Hyper-connected logistics ecosystems are also facilitating seamless collaboration between supply chain partners, allowing businesses to share real-time trade insights, demand forecasts, and inventory levels. Digital supply chain control towers act as centralized hubs where businesses can monitor logistics operations across multiple regions, predict supply chain bottlenecks, and automate decision-making processes based on AI-driven data insights.

10.2 The Emergence of Space Logistics and Its Impact on Global Trade

While logistics has traditionally been limited to earthbound supply chains, the emergence of space logistics and interplanetary trade is becoming an exciting reality. Advances in private space exploration, reusable rocket technology, and commercial space stations are paving the way for supply chain operations beyond Earth's atmosphere. Companies such as SpaceX, Blue Origin, and NASA are actively working on space cargo transportation, lunar supply chains, and asteroid mining logistics, opening new frontiers for logistics innovation.

One of the primary areas where space logistics will have a significant impact is satellite-enabled supply chain optimization. With the launch of thousands of low-Earth orbit (LEO) satellites, businesses can achieve unprecedented levels of global trade monitoring, real-time tracking, and predictive analytics. Satellite-powered logistics networks enhance global shipping route optimization, maritime freight tracking, and AI-driven logistics decision-making by providing continuous data feeds on supply chain movements, climate conditions, and trade bottlenecks.

Another breakthrough in space logistics is the development of off-world supply chain infrastructure. With plans for lunar colonies, Mars settlements, and space mining operations, logistics companies are exploring how to transport cargo, manage interplanetary inventory, and build autonomous freight solutions for extraterrestrial trade. NASA's Artemis program and SpaceX's Starship cargo missions are laying the groundwork for space-based logistics networks that will support human expansion beyond Earth.

Space logistics is also set to redefine global transportation speeds. Future advancements in hypersonic cargo delivery, space-based supply chain hubs, and point-to-point suborbital shipping could revolutionize international freight transportation. Hypersonic cargo planes, capable of traveling at speeds five times faster than commercial jets, could reduce ocean freight transit times from weeks to hours, drastically improving supply chain agility.

Another potential impact of space logistics is sustainable resource sourcing. Scientists and aerospace companies are exploring asteroid mining as a way to extract rare metals, minerals, and raw materials that are scarce on Earth but abundant in space. By tapping into space-based resources, industries can reduce reliance on Earth's depleting natural resources and create a new trade ecosystem beyond our planet.

Despite the exciting possibilities of space logistics, businesses must consider the regulatory, ethical, and environmental challenges associated with space-based supply chains. The cost of space transportation, legal ownership of extraterrestrial resources, and sustainability concerns will need to be addressed before space logistics can become a fully commercialized industry.

The logistics industry is evolving into a hyper-connected, AI-driven, and space-enabled ecosystem, where real-time data, automation, and sustainability shape the future of global trade. Businesses that embrace IoT-powered logistics networks, 5G connectivity, and AI-driven decision-making will gain a competitive advantage in optimizing supply chain efficiency, reducing costs, and improving service reliability.

Meanwhile, the emergence of space logistics and interplanetary trade opens unprecedented opportunities for global commerce, with potential breakthroughs in hypersonic cargo delivery, satellite-powered logistics tracking, and off-world supply chain networks. Companies that invest in space-based logistics technologies and satellite-driven trade insights will lead the industry into a new era of ultra-fast, intercontinental freight movement and off-Earth logistics expansion.

As logistics continues to transform at an exponential rate, businesses must remain agile, technologically advanced, and forward-thinking to stay ahead of global supply chain trends, emerging market opportunities, and future trade innovations. The future of logistics is no longer limited to Earth, it is expanding into the digital, hyper-connected, and space-driven economy of tomorrow.

REVIEWS

"This book is a game-changer for anyone in the logistics industry. Stella Eshett has taken an often-overlooked subject and made it engaging, insightful, and incredibly relevant to today's business landscape. The depth of research and the clarity of writing make this a must-read for professionals and entrepreneurs alike."

- **Ademola Akinyemi, Supply Chain Consultant, Lagos**

"Finally, a book that truly captures the essence of logistics! Stella Eshett does a fantastic job of breaking down complex supply chain concepts into easy-to-understand language. As someone who runs an e-commerce business, I found the chapters on last-mile delivery and global trade particularly valuable. Highly recommended!"

- **Chioma Okafor, Founder, SwiftCart Nigeria**

"What I love about this book is how it connects logistics to real-world applications. It doesn't just tell you how logistics works, it shows you how to leverage it for business success. The insights on AI, blockchain, and automation in supply chains are eye-opening. This is a book that should be on every business owner's shelf."

- **Uche Obi, Logistics Manager, Zenith Freight Services**

"Reading this book changed the way I view supply chains. It's easy to take logistics for granted until you see how much strategy and innovation go into making global trade possible. Stella Eshett's writing is engaging and informative, and the book offers practical knowledge that can be applied in both small and large businesses."

- **Fatima Adamu, Operations Director, Greenline Distributions**

"A brilliant exploration of logistics that blends technical expertise with real-world storytelling. Stella Eshett has written a book that not only educates but also inspires. If you want to understand how logistics will shape the future of business, this is the book to read."

- **Segun Alabi, Head of Logistics, West Africa Trade Hub**